Friendship Gifts

by Suzanne McNeill

LEISURE ARTS, INC.
and
OXMOOR HOUSE, INC.

Dedicated to my sister, Brendy Kilber and my mother, Lois Browne. Every year since I remember, our family has made gifts for family and friends. In my mother's famous words, "It's the thought that counts."

Credits

Art Director ❤ Janet Long ♡ Managing Director ❤ Kathy McMillan
Artists ❤ Patty Williams, Marti Wyble, Charlie Davis Young, Carol Van Ness
Friendship Editor ❤ Barbara Burnett ♡ Friendship Crafts ❤ Delores Frantz
Photographers ❤ David and Donna Thomason
Editors ❤ Mary Harrison, Wanda J. Little, Colleen Reigh

Printed in the United States of America
First Printing

Library of Congress
Catalog Card
Number 96-77251

Hardcover
ISBN 0-8487-1569-1

Softcover
ISBN 1-57486-056-9

Leisure Arts, Inc.
P.O. Box 55595
Little Rock, AR 72215

Friendship Gifts

by Suzanne McNeill

The best gifts are
the crafts someone made
especially for you. What you
create with your hands will be
treasured forever by the ones you love.

To: My
Special
Friend

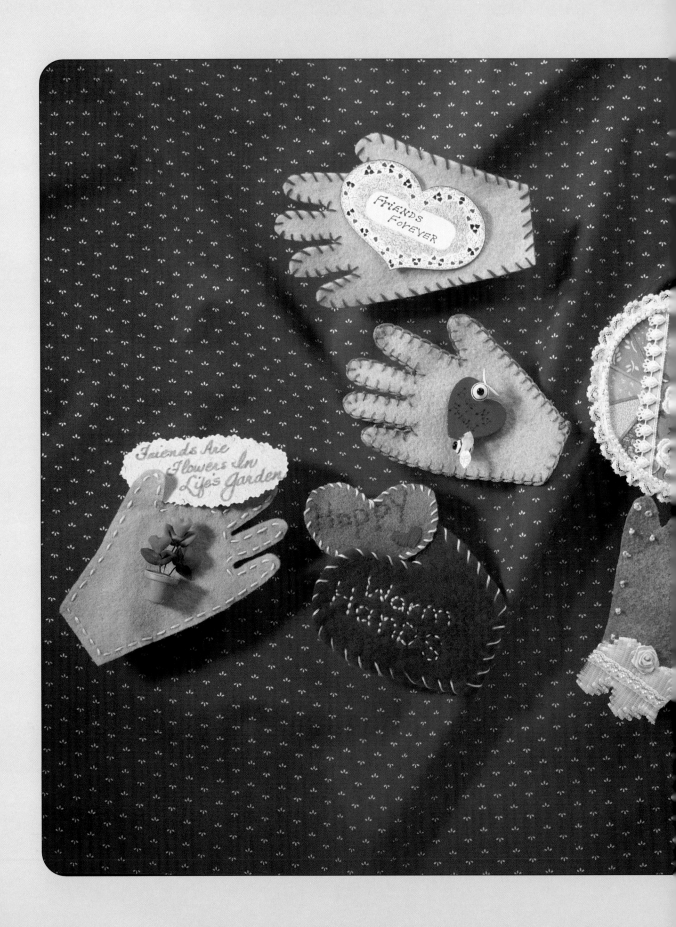

Table of Contents

Gifts of Friendship bring warm memories to cherish and a life blessed with the joys of giving...friend to friend.

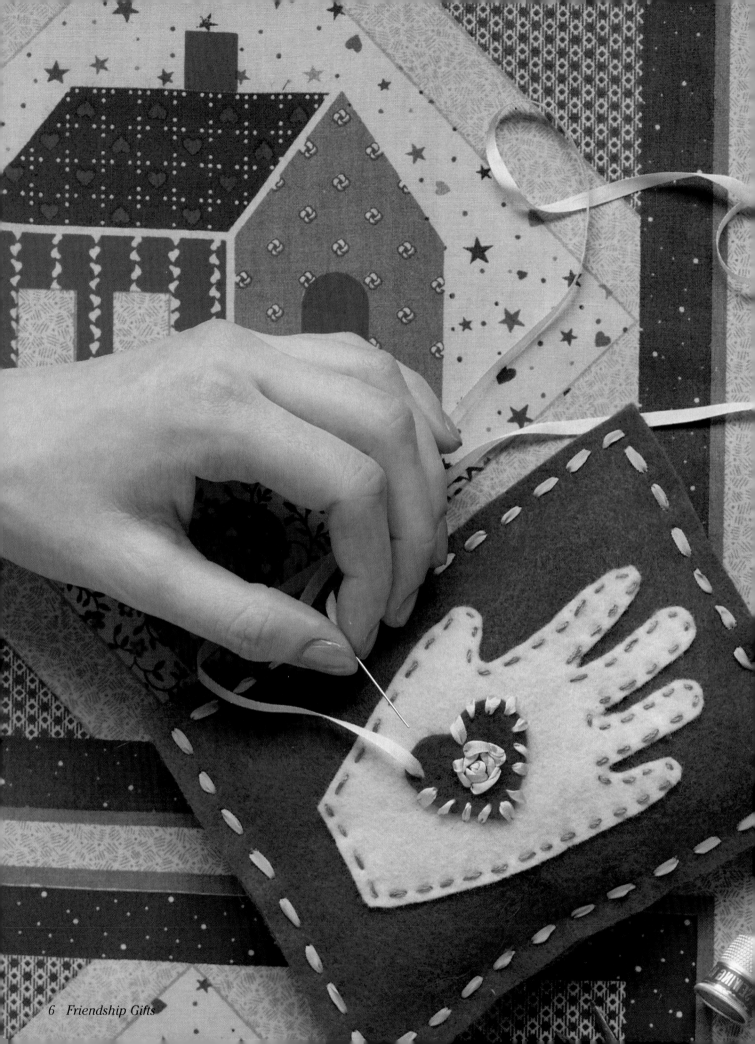

Friendship Gifts

There is no greater satisfaction than giving a gift to someone who has touched your life in a special way. Whether it is to brighten a friend's day, to say "you mean a lot," or just to put a smile on their face, nothing says more than a gift you have made with your own two hands. It says, "I care enough to spend time creating a one-of-a-kind gift just for you."

Each gift in this book is a celebration of fond friendship. Each relationship is unique and each gift reveals a peek into the bond with a loved one. What we value in our friends and how we express fond feelings through crafts is showcased here with heartwarming stories from the gift giver or recipient.

My mother always says,"The best gifts are the ones someone made especially for you. What you create with your hands will be treasured forever by the ones you love." To this day whenever I give a gift, it just has to be a gift from the heart...a gift that expresses a message of enduring friendship or a reminder of special moments we have shared. Even if minutes are precious, time spent crafting for friends is never wasted.

Robert Louis Stevenson said, "A friend is a gift we give ourselves." We choose our favorite friends on common grounds, interests and values. The institution of friendship requires no material expectations, no formal ceremonies and no enforceable laws...only someone who enjoys you and whom you enjoy.

Thank you to the friends who shared their stories of kindred friendships. I hope their rich experiences of life will inspire women everywhere to ignite the flame of friendship and reap the rewards that only come from giving a handmade gift.

Suzanne

Suzanne McNeill

One step into Suzanne McNeill's home and you know a craft lover lives here. Handmade treasures...souvenirs of her travels around the world are displayed everywhere. From a painted leather dreamcatcher 'Spirit Shield', to a colorful embroidered child's shirt, pants and belt from Guatemala, Suzanne admires the handiwork of all cultures.

"I'm baking orange slice - oatmeal - coconut cookies," she explained. "I hope you don't mind." Suzanne McNeill founder of **Design Originals** 'how-to' craft publishing company has definitely captured the magic of crafting. A lifetime of creating has not only imparted a wealth of knowledge, but a rewarding career doing something she loves.

In 1984 Suzanne found herself a single mother with four children to raise. With a baby on her knee, she began designing needlework patterns. That first year, she published only four books. Her daughter Lani and a friend Linda helped fill orders from one end of their dining room table.

Since 1984, with the help of creative friends and designers from all across the country, Suzanne has published over 400 craft 'how-to' books. Today with a world wide distribution network, **Design Originals** is well respected and highly regarded with industry leaders and crafters of all ages.

On any given day you may find Suzanne watching an Indian mother pass down the art of basket weaving in a small village along the Equator, baking orange slice cookies in her cozy country kitchen, playing softball with her church team, backpacking in Colorado, rafting down the Grand Canyon or overseeing designs and ideas for new books.

Her calm demeanor belies her energy, sense of adventure and entrepreneurial spirit. Handmade treasures from friends and collections of folk art fill every room of her home. Fanciful carved and painted wooden Oaxacan 'animales' from Mexico peer down from high shelves. Woven Mayan 'huipil' shirts grace a painted ladder from Santa Fe. Hand looped

carryall bags from Ecuador grace a small hall table. A Zhostovo lacquered black tray painted with Russian florals is elegantly displayed on a dining room wall.

Crafting has colored Suzanne's life from a very early age. She learned from her mother the simple pleasures of making something by hand. Her great grandmother taught her to embroider...little horses at the age of 6. One of her earliest recollections was of her mother hooking a rug from her father's outgrown wool suits. Her grandmother taught her to sew on a treadle machine. Today, that same old sewing machine lives in perfect harmony as a table with her more recent and eclectic possessions.

The resourcefulness Suzanne acquired early in life served her well when she became a single mother. With a desire to stay home with her children and earn a living too, she began working at her dining room table designing freelance patterns. Discouraged by the lengthy lead time between submission and acceptance, Suzanne struck out on her own and published four books under the **Design Originals** label. As her children grew, so did her company.

Suzanne credits her success not only to her mother who taught her the love of crafting, but to living by her favorite motto, "Find a job you love and you will never work another day in your life!" Although she considers herself, "just a craftsperson who just happens to be in business," the savvy entrepreneur has answered every knock on the window of opportunity.

Every day Suzanne receives "friendship notes" from crafters. Each encouraging and kind note is filed for safe keeping. It's where Suzanne often goes to find renewal when a creative boost is needed. With every story she reads about how crafting has filled a void in someone's life, brought happiness or comfort to the sick or needy because of the generosity of crafting volunteers, inspired others to feel good about themselves, or made a child smile with pride, she knows that crafting is what she wants to be doing.

Suzanne considers herself truly blessed. A lifelong love of crafts has afforded her the opportunity to share with the rest of the world through her books, an inquisitive spirit, a thirst for knowledge and the love of crafting.

Barbara Burnett

*M*y mom Teresa, has been both mother and father to me since I was 6 weeks old. In spite of financial hardships, she was determined I would go to college. Because of her perseverance I am attending the University of Tennessee on a full football scholarship. "Thanks mom for always believing in me. Thanks for giving me my roots and my wings."

Joey Barczak

My mom deserves hugs and kisses.

Once in a lifetime,
you find someone special.

I often think my friend
Judi (bottom) knows me
even better than I know
myself. She has helped me to
achieve my personal goals
as a strong person and creative designer. I created this
crochet brooch in gratitude
for Judi's caring heart and
unshakeable friendship.

Mary Jo Hiney

When Kim (left) and I heard Suzanne McNeill loved pandas and pigs, it seemed the perfect thank you gift. Suzanne published my first book on clay several years ago and since then I have continued to design for her. Every book is as exciting as the first.

Connie Riepl

When you are kindred spirits, friendships are even more special. It took mutual friends to introduce Connie Riepl and me. It wasn't long before we became partners in a crafting business. We love getting together several times a year to sell our creations at shows.

Sue Brunner

TO TWO I LOVE

When I stop to count my blessings
As I often try to do,
Among my joys and thankfulness
Are happy thoughts of you.

And Sisters, you're so very near
The inmost self of me,
You know what hurts, what helps..
The needs I have,
You are so very dear.

We're not as one on everything,
Opinionated we!
But eye to eye and heart to heart
On what matters, we agree.

We've traveled many a highway
A singin' as we go,
Our voices blend old songs or new
With harmony all our own.

A wealth of memories we share
A heritage precious, too,
This world a poorer place would be
Without the two of you.

FOR PUSH WITH LOVE BY LORAINE 1992

SISTER

Every child is a 'heaven scent' angel. This Heaven Scent Sock Angel was made for a very special baby - the grandchild of a good friend. I left the sock tucked in so the angel will stand and so the potpourri can be changed or freshened. . . from Judy (second from right).

Judy LaSalle

Daughters of preacher Slater, who wrote hymns and taught singing, sisters Loraine (left), Ruth (center) and Thelma (right) sang and performed together for parties and weddings all their lives.

Thelma wrote this poem expressing her love. Loraine cross stitched four copies of the poem... for herself, as a memorial for Ruth, and two for Thelma's children.

Thelma Banowsky & Loraine Scott

'Friends Are Love' Shingle

PHOTO ON PAGES 10-11
MATERIALS:
5" x 17" redwood shingle
1/16" balsa wood sticks
3/4" wood heart
7 small sunflowers with leaves
Baby's breath, 24" of 18 gauge wire
Lo-temp hot and White glues
2 thumbtacks, Natural raffia
Clear acrylic spray sealer, Craft knife
INSTRUCTIONS:

1. Wrap wire around a pencil to curl. Remove and stretch leaving loops and bends. Bend a small loop on each end and tack to corners on back of shingle.

2. Cut balsa wood. Glue wood letters on shingle with White glue. Glue heart above the I. Spray plaque with sealer. Referring to photo, glue leaves and flowers on plaque.

Crochet Rose Brooch

PHOTO ON PAGE 12
by Mary Jo Hiney
MATERIALS:
5/8 yard of 1½" Ivory wired ribbon
3 crochet flower doilies (2½", 3½", 4")
1½" bar pin, Package of White stamens
Ivory sewing thread, Needle
GOOP glue, Hot glue
INSTRUCTIONS:

Ruffle - Cut 7" of ribbon, fold in half matching cut ends. Stitch or glue a ¼" seam along cut ends. Open ribbon seam side out and gather stitch along one long edge. Pull gathers as tight as possible and secure thread. Trim or fold stamens if necessary then glue to center of ruffle.

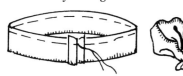

Glue 2½" doily to bottom of ribbon ruffle pinching doily at base so it ruffles slightly. Glue 3½" doily to bottom of previous layer, pinching doily at base to ruffle. Repeat with 4" doily.

Fold and stitch 3 pointed petal leaves and glue to back of flower. Glue pin back to center back of pin near the top. Cut a

1½" piece of ribbon and fold under the cut ends. Glue over base of pin back for a clean finish.

'Light up my Life' Candle

PHOTO ON PAGE 12
MATERIALS:
13" Bendi Doll
2½" x 6" glass container
Blonde doll hair
20" of ½" tea dyed lace
20" of 3" Natural straw ribbon
1⅔ yards of 1/8" Taupe ribbon
¼ yard of Beige print fabric
3" x 5" of Red print fabric
3" x 5" of HeatnBond™
Toothpick
Red paint writer
Red and Taupe acrylic paint
White glue and GOOP glue

INSTRUCTIONS:

Paint smile Red and slippers Taupe. Cut two 24" pieces of ribbon. Center and glue one piece on bottom of each foot. Wrap ribbon around legs crossing twice in front and twice in back. Tie ends in a bow. Place a dot of glue on center of bow. Body Suit - Cut a 4½" x 6" piece of Beige fabric. Fold both long edges under ¼". Wrap fabric around doll's body. Overlap at back and glue. Pull fabric together at crotch and glue.

Skirt - Cut a 4½" x 26" piece of Beige fabric. Pull threads out and fringe one long edge. Fold fabric in half lengthwise

with right sides together. Glue 4½" edges together. Fold top edge under ¼". Sew a gathering stitch along top edge. Slip skirt on doll, gather and tie ends to secure.

Sleeves - Cut a ½" x 6" piece of Beige fabric. Pull out threads and fringe one 6" edge. Fold other 6" edge under ¼". Sew a gathering stich along this edge. Place gathered sleeve over shoulder and glue to top edge of body suit at the front and back. Repeat for other sleeve.

Lace - Cut 6" of lace. Starting at the waist in front, glue lace up the front of the body suit, over the shoulder and down to waist at back. Repeat for other side. Glue an 8" piece of lace around waist covering the skirt gathers.

Hair - Fluff and spread out a long strand of hair. Glue to top and sides of head. Pull hair across back of the head and bunch it over the shoulder. Knot a 9" piece of ribbon around hair and tie ends in a bow. Glue ribbon rose in center of bow.

Wings - Using pattern, cut 2 wings from straw ribbon. Run a fine line of White glue around edges of wings to prevent fraying. Crush each wing together at its center. Place wings side by side and tie together with a piece of ribbon. Glue wings just below doll's neck.

Wand - Following manufacturer's instructions, apply HeatnBond to the wrong side of two 3" squares of Red fabric. Bond one piece to poster board. Draw star pattern on paper side of second piece and cut out star. Remove paper backing. Place star on bonded poster board. Place tip of a toothpick between star and poster board, bond layers together. Cut around star.

Wrap doll around container. Tie legs in a knot. Use GOOP to glue hands to container. Place wand in one hand. Use tape to hold hands in place until glue dries. Use the paint writer to letter 'You Light Up My Life' on container.

Note: Use only votive candles in container. Light candle carefully avoiding contact with the doll.

WING PATTERN

Pig & Panda Pins

PHOTO ON PAGE 13

by Connie Riepl

MATERIALS:

Flesh, White, Red, Black oven bake clay
Two 1" pin backs, Black acrylic paint
Paintbrush, Pink cosmetic blush
Cotton swab, GOOP glue
Toothpick, Small thin bladed knife
Cookie sheet, Home oven

PIG INSTRUCTIONS:

Body - Using Flesh clay, roll a 1" teardrop, place on cookie sheet and flatten back. Roll a ½" ball for head, press on body. For legs and arms roll 1" long cylinders ⅜" in diameter. Press on body and flatten back. Roll ⅜" balls, flatten and press on head for ears. Shape a small piece of clay for snout, press on head. Make nostrils, belly button, eyes and eyebrows with toothpick.

Bow - Roll Red clay very thin, cut two ¾" pieces for bow streamers and two ⅜" pieces for bow. Press streamers on neck. Fold bow pieces in half, press on streamers. Roll a tiny ball, press in center of bow. Cut heart from Red, press on pig.

Finish - Bake pig following manufacturer's instructions, cool. Paint hooves and eyes Black. Rub cheeks with blush. Glue pin on back.

PANDA INSTRUCTIONS:

Body - Using White clay, roll a 1" teardrop, place on cookie sheet and flatten back. Roll a ½" ball for head, press on body. For legs and arms roll Black 1" long cylinders ⅜" in diameter. Press on body and flatten back. Roll Black ⅜" balls, flatten and press on head for ears. Shape a small piece of White clay for snout, press on head. Roll a tiny Black ball for nose. Make fur marks, mouth line, eyes and eyebrows with toothpick.

Bow - Roll Red clay very thin. Cut two ¾" pieces for bow streamers and two ⅜" pieces for bow. Press streamers on neck. Fold bow pieces in half, press on streamers. Roll a tiny ball, press in center of bow. Cut heart from Red, press on bear.

Finish - Bake panda bear following manufacturer's instructions, cool. Paint eyes Black. Rub cheeks with blush. Glue pin on back.

HEART PATTERN

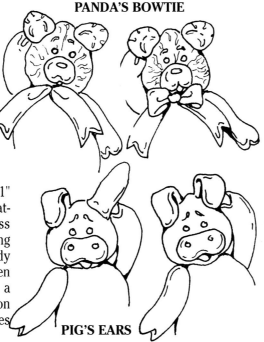

PANDA'S BOWTIE

PIG'S EARS

'Somebunny Loves You'

PHOTO ON PAGE 13

by Sue Brunner

MATERIALS:

5" jointed rabbit
6" of ⅛" Pink satin ribbon
1" wood heart, Pink acrylic paint
Paintbrush, 1" clay pot
Black fine tip permanent marker
Red, Pink, Brown, Green oven bake clay
Non stick cooking spray, Cookie sheet
6" of Green floral wire, Home oven

INSTRUCTIONS:

Form 2 Pink and 1 Red heart flowers, 3 Green leaves and Brown ball to fit in pot. Press leaves on flowers. Cut 1" to 1½" wire stems. Insert stems in flowers and ball. Place arrangement on cookie sheet covered with nonstick spray. Bake following clay manufacturer's instructions.

Bend rabbit into a sitting position and glue hips to secure. Tie a ribbon bow and glue on head. Paint heart Pink. Write 'Somebunny Loves You' with marker. Glue flowers in pot, gluepot to one arm and heart to other arm.

PATTERN

'Heaven Scent' Sock Angel

PHOTO ON PAGE 14

by Judy LaSalle

MATERIALS:

Child's Pink nylon sock
Rubber band
18" of 5" White eyelet lace
⅓ cup of potpourri
7" round White Battenburg lace doily
5 small Mauve roses with wire stems
12" of ¼" Mauve satin ribbon
Cosmetic blush
Black embroidery floss
Needle and thread
Polyester fiberfill
Hot glue

INSTRUCTIONS:

Body - Stuff sock with fiberfill pushing potpourri into center. Push cuff up into sock. Wrap rubber band one third of the way from top to indicate neck. Make French knot eyes with Black floss.

Dress - With needle and thread, gather top of eyelet around neck and secure at back.

Wings - Gather center of doily, tie off securely. Glue to back of neck.

Finish - Brush blush under eyes for cheeks. Tie ribbon bow, glue to front of neck. Twist stems of roses together, glue to top of head for halo.

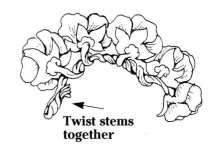

Twist stems together

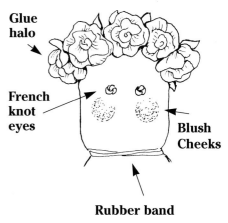

Glue halo

French knot eyes

Blush Cheeks

Rubber band

Cross Stitch Poem

PHOTO ON PAGE 14

*by Thelma Banowsky
and Loraine Scott*

MATERIALS:

12½" x 17" Mauve frame
with glass

12½" x 17" Mauve mat
with 8¾" x 13¼"
opening

12½" x 17" Dark Mauve
mat with 8" x 12½"
opening

12½" x 17" cardboard
backing

12½" x 17" of 18 count
Ivory aida cloth

Size 26 tapestry needle

Embroidery floss

Violet

Medium Baby Green

Medium Yellow

Delft Blue

Peach Flesh

Tangerine

Cranberry

INSTRUCTIONS:

Fold cloth in fourths
to find center. Beginning
at center and following
chart, stitch words, bor-
der and corner motifs.
Iron cloth flat. Mat and
frame poem referring to
photo.

● 553 Violet

— 966 Medium Baby
Green

○ 743 Medium Yellow

X 809 Delft Blue

△ 353 Peach Flesh

•. 742 Light Tangerine

II 740 Tangerine

M 603 Cranberry

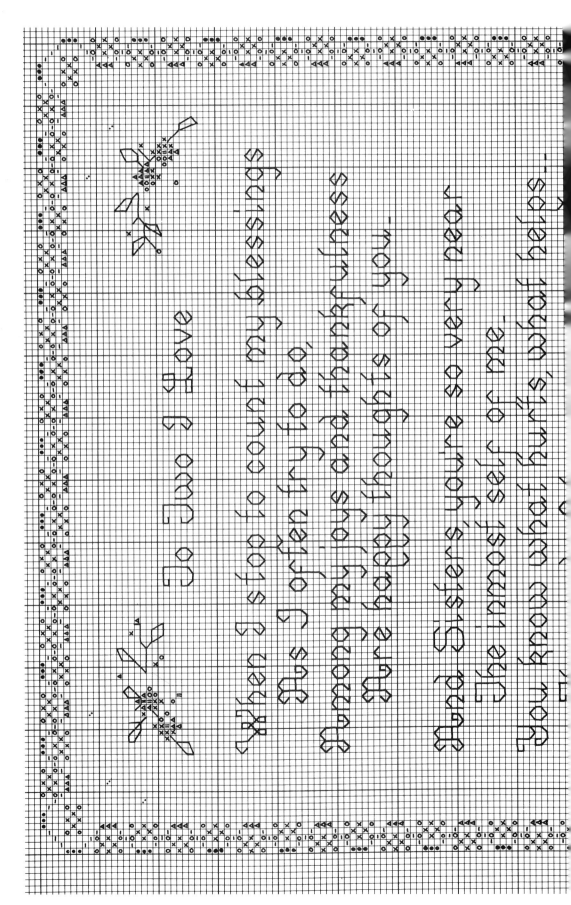

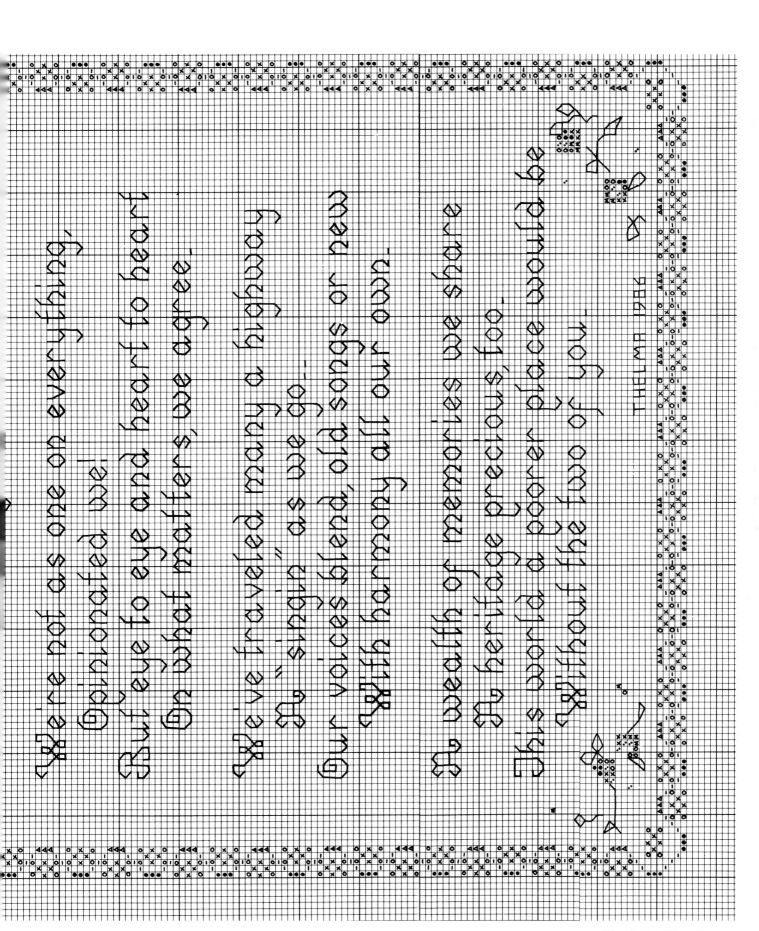

We are not as one on everything,
But eye to eye and heart to heart
On what matters, we agree –

We've traveled many a highway,
Of age so separate –
Our voices blend, old songs or new,
With harmony all our own –

A wealth of memories we share
A heritage precious too –
This world would be bereft
Without the two of you –

THELMA 1984

I made this sampler to give to my daughter, Genevieve (right), who is my best friend. I chose this gift for her because she has just entered high school and has begun to gather memories that will last her a lifetime. As she begins to blossom into a woman and develops a caring attitude toward life, she will brighten our lives together as mother and daughter and as special friends, giving us memories as long as we live.

Vickie Lee Dean

I give this with my own special touch.

I designed this special pin for my good friend Susan (left) on the occasion of her wedding. The locket is to hold photos of the couple, the "S" is from some old jewelry of Susan's. The "Kiss" is because she is in love with chocolate! The photo of us was taken on her wedding day.

Darlene Keefe

Share your creativity with friends.

Friends from the start - as sisters we will never part. As children my sister Tammy (right) and I loved playing in Grandma's button box. Everytime she wears this button necklace I hope it brings back the wonderful memories of Grandma.

Dana Bemboom

Bryce (left), my best friend in college, will always hold a special place in my heart. Over the years we have enjoyed exchanging small sentimental gifts. I made this miniature beaded bag for Bryce to hold all the special memories of our friendship.

Lani Stiles

Paula Amador (left) and I became acquainted in a most unlikely place, a doctor's office. As the receptionist, Paula always has a ready smile and great sense of humor. Our friendship began with typical doctor's office small talk. Paula's favorite color is purple, so I knew she would like this handmade necklace set.

Patty Williams

This little pin was made for my special friend Jean. She is always there to plant a loving foot in the middle of my back and give me a gentle PUSH whenever I drag behind. I like her because she is a woman with strong opinions. To me she is The Queen!... from Kim (center)

Kim Ballor

My granddaughter, Jessica (right), loves to play and work with my beads. On her last visit, she wanted to make something really special for her mom, Karin. She chose the red beads and gold chain and together we made a vintage style necklace that was a perfect accent for her mom's favorite dress.

Wanda J. Little

All you need is love.

My daughter, Nancy, and I are very close friends. She is married now and lives 1000 miles away. When her first child was born, she sent me a photo of him in a hand decorated frame. Each year on his birthday she sends a new one. This year I will be receiving two framed photographs - one of Phillip and one of his new little brother Sammy.

Linda Rocamontes

When I first saw these great antique charms, I knew my friend Pam (left) would love them. We like to browse antique and flea markets together, so I made this beautiful lapel pin just for her.

Barbara Shirley

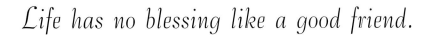

Life has no blessing like a good friend.

Memories Sampler

PHOTO ON PAGES 20-21
by Vickie Lee Dean

MATERIALS:

15" x 17" piece of Osnaburg fabric
16" x 18" of Red checked fabric
1 fabric yo-yo
2 heart buttons
5 large and 6 small antique buttons
Embroidery floss -
  Forest Green
  Dark Red
Disappearing fabric marker
6" x 18" Dark Green frame
Hot glue

Optional: Tea bags

INSTRUCTIONS:

Fray edges of Osnaburg. Using fabric marker, print 'Memories we collect and give brighten our lives as long as we live.' Letters should be childlike and need not be perfect. Back stitch with Forest Green floss.

Center Red checked fabric under Osnaburg. Using Dark Red floss, make long running stitches ½" from outer edges of Osnaburg attaching it to Red checked fabric.

Sew or glue 4 large buttons to each corner and one large button to bottom center of Osnaburg. Glue or sew yo-yo to top center. Cut out 2 small hearts, attach with running stitches to each side of yo-yo. Sew or glue 2 heart buttons to outer side of hearts and 6 small buttons scattered over hearts and yo-yo.

Optional: To antique sampler, brew strong tea. Soak sampler in tea until desired color is reached, remove from tea, iron flat.

Place sampler in frame.

Seamstress Tools

PHOTO ON PAGES 20-21
by Lois Browne

MATERIALS:

1 yard of 1" Red/Black woven ribbon
1 yard of 1" Red grosgrain Ribbon
20" of ⅜" Red grosgrain ribbon
Small tomato pin cushion
Small pair of scissors, 2" x 3" of suede
Thimble, Straight pins

INSTRUCTIONS:

Fold suede in half to measure 2" x 1½". Sew a ¼" seam on one side. Place 1" Red ribbon behind woven ribbon and sew along long edges with matching thread, catching open edge of suede between ribbon layers 3" from one end.

Cut 8" of ⅜" ribbon, slip through handles of scissors and sew ends to one end of wide ribbon. Cut remaining ⅜" ribbon in half and wrap pieces around pin cushion, equally dividing it into fourths. Sew the 4 ends of ⅜" ribbon to other end of wide ribbon.

Place thimble in suede pocket and pins in cushion. Place ribbon around neck to use.

ADD
SCISSORS
HERE

Collage Friendship Pin

PHOTO ON PAGE 22   *by Darlene Keefe*
MATERIALS:

Small pearl button, Novelty kiss charm
Initial charm, 6mm Gold jumpring
Small novelty sticker, Silver paint pen
Black acrylic paint, Paintbrush
Acrylic spray varnish, Rubbing alcohol
E6000 glue, Paper towels, Wire cutters
Needle nose pliers

BRASS CHARMS:
Base, Connector, Cherub,
Two corners, Pin back
Rose, Frame, Frame Back,
Locket, 'I Love You'

CLAMP FRAME

INSTRUCTIONS:

1. Clean charms with alcohol to remove oil and dirt. Paint charms with Black acrylic paint and wipe off with paper towel leaving paint in crevices for a soft antique look. Let dry. Paint rose and kiss Silver. Let dry. Spray charms with 2 light coats of varnish to seal.

2. Cut loops off all charms except locket and leave center loop on connector. Cut lower branches off rose.

3. Glue initial to locket. Let dry. Glue connector to bottom edge of base with loop down. Let dry.

4. Attach sticker to frame back, insert back in frame. Clamp edges of frame to secure (do not to bend frame).

Assemble - Attach charms and button to base in layers with small dabs of glue . Let dry between layers. Attach locket to connector with jumpring. Allow pin to dry completely. Glue pin to top of back.

Note - Small amounts of glue dry in 1 hour, larger amounts can take up to 24 hours. A flat toothpick may be helpful in applying small amounts of glue.

and give ♡

long as we live

Button Necklace

PHOTO ON PAGE 22

by Dana Bemboom

Wrap 5 times →

Open eye pin

MATERIALS:
27" Gold chain
Gold clasp
6mm jumpring
29 eye pins
Beads : two 6mm Amber
  Two 8mm Amber
  9mm Green Iridescent flat
  9mm x 13mm Amber cylinder
  4mm x 10mm Blue cylinder
  4mm x 14mm Black striped cylinder
Brass charms (Sewing machine with
  loop, 5 spools, 3 swan scissors,
  4 thimbles)
¾" buttons (2 White & 2 Brown pearl)
⅝" buttons (2 Blue, 2 Pink, 2 Lavender,
  2 Navy Blue, 2 Tan)
½" buttons (Pink, Blue, Green)
Wire cutters, Round nose pliers
GOOP glue

INSTRUCTIONS:

Sewing Machine - Find center of chain, attach sewing machine charm to chain with jumpring. Cut loop off one spool charm with wire cutters. Glue spool, Green and Tan buttons on sewing machine referring to photo.

Clasp - For each Blue button, thread an eye pin through each hole leaving a ¼" space between eye pin loop and button. Wrap ends of pin 5 times around ¼" space and cut off excess. Open eye pin loops and attach one to chain and one to clasp, close loops.

Button Dangles - Make button dangles with remaining buttons. Thread an eye pin through one hole leaving a ¼" space between eye pin loop and button. Wrap end of pin 5 times around ¼" and cut off excess.

Bead Dangles - Thread an eye pin though each bead, cut end to ¼" and make loop with round nose pliers. Open bottom loops and referring to photo attach charms.

Assemble - Space charms on chain at 1" intervals, open top loops of dangles and attach charms to chain. Attach loop on sewing machine.

Lariat Necklace

PHOTO ON PAGE 23

by Patty Williams

MATERIALS:
10" of White/Silver cord
3 Silver 6mm jumprings
2 Silver crimps
Silver lobster claw clasp
3 Silver prong bell caps
2 Silver fishhook ear wires
GOOP glue, Needle nose pliers, Scissors
Dark Amethyst faceted acrylic beads
  (three 13mm x 10mm squatty bicone,
  three 32mm x 9mm pendants)

INSTRUCTIONS:

1. Place a drop of glue inside each bell cap, insert pendants and close cap around pendant with pliers. Let dry.
2. For necklace, attach a jumpring to 1 of the bell caps.
3. Thread 10" of cord through a jumpring, thread on 1 bead. Glue cord and bead as shown in diagram. Let dry.
4. Tie overhand knots on each strand of cord, add beads and tie overhand knots above each bead.
5. Before adding clasp, try on necklace and mark cord length needed.
6. Attach crimps to each end of cord and add jumprings to each crimp

bead using pliers. Attach clasp to one of the jumprings.

Earrings - Attach pendants to ear wires.

> *Make necklaces and earrings for your family and friends using the appropriate birthstone.*
>
> | | |
> |---|---|
> | *Jan. - Garnet* | *Feb. - Amethyst* |
> | *Mar. - Aquamarine* | *Apr. - Diamond* |
> | *May - Emerald* | *June - Pearl* |
> | *July - Ruby* | *Aug. - Peridot* |
> | *Sept. - Sapphire* | *Oct.- Opal* |
> | *Nov. - Topaz* | *Dec. - Turquoise* |

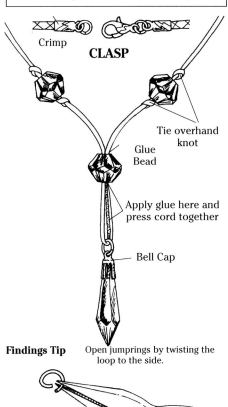

Crimp

CLASP

Tie overhand knot

Glue Bead

Apply glue here and press cord together

Bell Cap

Open jumprings by twisting the loop to the side.

Findings Tip

Open earwires and jumprings

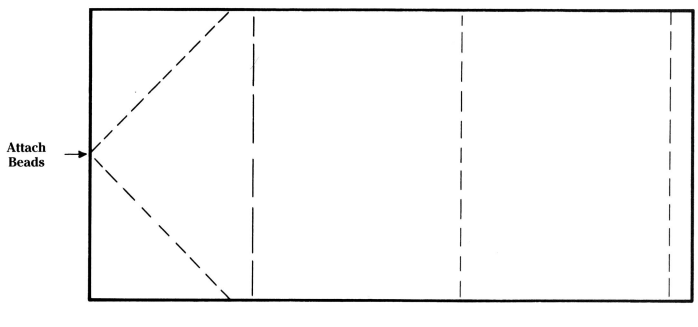

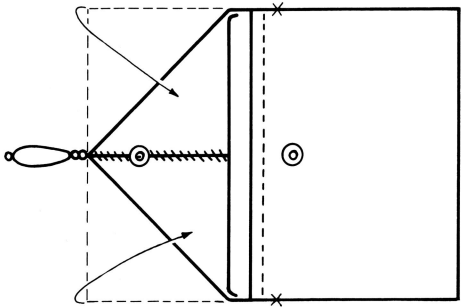

Purple Iridescent Seed

9 mm Green Bugle

15 mm Green Long

Mauve Bugle

Mauve Rochaille

Bag Fringe

BAG STRAP - Reverse and Repeat - Repeat 7 more times

Beaded Bag Necklace

PHOTO ON PAGE 23
by Lani Stiles
MATERIALS:

6½" of brocade wire edge ribbon
Hunter Green thread, sewing needle
White beading thread, beading needle
Small snap, Tigertail, 2 crimp beads
Needle nose pliers

BEADS:

35mm Mauve bugle beads
9mm Green bugle beads
Mauve rochaille seed beads
Purple Iridescent seed beads
2 Green 15mm long beads
25mm Green teardrop beads

INSTRUCTIONS:

Bag - Turn under one cut end of

ribbon ¼", turn under again and stitch. Measure 2¼" from hemmed edge, fold up to form bottom edge. Whip stitch sides together. Fold top to form a pointed flap and stitch. Sew snap parts to point of flap and to front of bag.

Fringe - Thread needle with beading thread, knot end and pass needle through center of bag bottom from inside to outside. String beads for fringe following fringe beading diagram. Evenly spacing stands on right and left sides of center strand. String beads for flap fringe following flap beading diagram.

Strap - To make loop to attach strap, string crimp bead and 6 Purple seed beads on tigertail, pass end of tigertail through one side seam of bag, add 6 Purple beads, pass through crimp, pull

beads snug and flatten crimp with pliers. String beads for strap following beading diagram. Attach to other side of bag with loop of Purple seed beads and a crimp bead.

'The Queen' Pin

PHOTO ON PAGE 24

by Kim Ballor

MATERIALS:

4" square of 300# watercolor paper
Mary Engelbreit 'The Queen' sticker
Decoupage finish
Clear spray glaze
Gold metallic paint
6 Gold head pins
6 Gold 5mm jumprings
3 Red 20mm bugle beads
3 Gold 25mm bugle beads
3 Red 3mm rhinestones
Pin back
Scissors
Needle nose pliers
Flat brush
Wire cutters
Hot glue
Small nail

INSTRUCTIONS:

1. Brush a coat of decoupage finish on the back of sticker, press firmly on watercolor paper. Brush a coat of finish over the top of the sticker, let dry. Cut out sticker. Make 6 holes in the bottom edge of sticker with a nail.
2. Trace crown pattern, cut from watercolor paper. Paint crown Gold, let dry.
3. Spray crown and sticker with decoupage glaze. Set rhinestones on crown while glaze is wet, let dry.
4. Dangles - Make 3 dangles by threading a Gold bugle bead on a head pin and 3 more dangles by threading a Gold bead and a Red bugle bead on a head pin. Trim ends of head pins to ¼". Make a loop on end of each pin by holding the end with pliers and rolling the end down. Attach dangles to hole in sticker with jumprings.
5. Glue crown to upper left corner and pin to upper back.

Crown Pattern

Vintage Necklace

PHOTO ON PAGE 24

by Wanda J. Little

MATERIALS:

24" of fine Gold chain
Red glass beads (2 each of 10mm disk, 8mm round, 6mm round)
10mm x 12mm Red glass teardrop bead
5 Gold eye pins
2 Gold head pins
12 Gold 6mm jumprings
Wire cutters
Round nose pliers

INSTRUCTIONS:

Beads - Thread head pins through 6mm beads, trim ends to ⅜" and bend in a loop. Thread eye pins through remaining beads, trims ends to ⅜" and bend in a loop.

Chain - Cut 1" and 1¼" pieces of chain, attach one end of each piece to a 6mm bead and other end to narrow part of teardrop using jumprings. Cut four 3" pieces of chain. On each side of necklace, attach one piece of chain to teardrop and disk bead and other piece to disk bead and 8mm bead with jumprings. Attach 9" of chain to 8mm beads.

Open jumprings to the side.

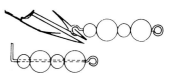

Use needlenose pliers to attach headpins and eyepins.

Cherub Frame

PHOTO ON PAGE 25

by Linda Rocamontes

MATERIALS:

2" x 3" hanging frame
GOOP glue

BRASS CHARMS:

1½" left facing Brass cherub
1½" right facing Brass cherub
2 Brass corners
18mm x 25mm Brass cabochon mount
18mm x 25mm angel cabochon

INSTRUCTIONS:

Glue cabochon in mount and glue to one Brass corner. Referring to photo, glue corners and cherubs on frame.

Raphael Angel Pin

PHOTO ON PAGE 25

by Barbara Shirley

BRASS CHARMS:

filigree
Two cherubs
Watchful cherub' stone
1" barpin

INSTRUCTIONS:

Glue cherubs to front of filigree and barpin to back of pin.

BURPEE
RADISH
Crimson Giant
NET WT. 4 g
All Things Grow With Love
Friendship Is Like A Garden... Both Need

*W*hen I needed a fancy dress to attend a formal function and was low on funds, I found a thrift store dress that was the right price, but needed some major alterations. My good friends, Sue (right) and Gail (top) completely remade the dress to fit me. When I walked out the door that night I felt like a million dollars. In fact, I met my future husband that night!

Sandy Rogers

Plant your seeds all in a row.

My mom, Suzanne (right), is a crafter and appreciates handmade gifts. This simple to make massager is a useful tool and I had great fun making it for her.

Todd Stiles

Friendship is a Blessing.

My friend Barbara (left) is a horticulture enthusiast and a bunny collector. As a thoughtful gift after she helped me through a taxing period, I made her this little bunny watering can and filled it with a mixed bouquet of her favorite fresh flowers. After the flowers' beauty had passed, I created a silk flower arrangement to put in its place so the flowers, like our friendship, will always be in bloom.

Jean Kievlan

I am so lucky that Todd, the 'love of my life' is also my best friend. Our relationship is based on mutual admiration, sharing and support of each other's hopes and dreams for the future.

This plant poke is one of many friendship gifts to be given throughout our lives together. From the seeds of friendship, love has grown.

Leizl Garma

Beverly is more than a sister to me. She is my best friend and confidant. Even though we live many miles apart and I rarely get to see her, we still exchange little gifts and call each other often. This sunflower in a pot represents how much she brightens my life.

Phyllis Kinnison

I made this little birdhouse pin for my friend Jennifer (right) who now 'nests' far from where our friendship began. I think of her every time I see the home of one of our feathered friends.
Cindy Bush Cambier

Part of the fun of making things is to share those things with family and friends.

We make this 'Friends Gather Here' sign to give to longtime friends who are the treasures of life to remind them of how special and precious they are. The sign could cheer them on a rainy day, remind them of good times and let them know that the door is always open. Or we give it as a welcome to a new friend who adds spice to our lives . . . from Denise (left) to JoAnn Wolfe (right).

Shirley Baer,
Dianna Koller,
Denise Basinger

Friendship is the meaning of life.

My friend, Frankie Appling (left), and I love to hunt through thrift shops and rummage sales for vintage linens, silverplate and china. Our gifts to each other allow us to become really creative. For Frankie's birthday, I made her a 'low calorie' cake from moss and flowers and I cut a slice for us to share. Of all the things we create, we value our memories the most.

Indrani Hawkins

...Friendship...Friendship...Friendship...
Friendship Is Like A Garden...Both Need War

HEART
CUT 2
RED

WATERING CAN
CUT 2
REVERSE 1
LIGHT BLUE

STEMS
CUT 10
REVERSE 5
GREEN

All Things
Grow With Love

Gardener's Tool Box

PHOTO ON PAGES 30-31

MATERIALS FOR GLOVES:

White cotton gardening gloves
Green, Light Blue and Red fabric scraps
10 assorted buttons
HeatnBond™
Black fabric marker
GOOP glue
Transfer paper
Household iron

MATERIALS FOR TOTE:

6½" x 12" wood tote
3 seed packets
Spade and fork
Small clay pot of flowers
24 assorted buttons
35 craft sticks
48 craft picks
Floral picks
Raffia
2 blocks of floral foam
Sand paper
Acrylic paint (Light Blue, Dark Green,
    Cream, Bright Green)

Paintbrush
Clear acrylic matte spray finish
Black fine tip permanent marker
Hack saw with fine blade
GOOP glue
Spanish moss

INSTRUCTIONS:

Gloves

Following manufacturer's instructions, iron HeatnBond on wrong side of fabrics. Trace patterns and transfer 10 flower stems, 2 hearts and 2 watering cans to paper side of HeatnBond matching fabric colors and flopping patterns for 1 watering can and 5 flower stems. Cut out shapes, remove paper backing and iron shapes on gloves referring to photo. Glue buttons to tops of stems. Write 'All Things Grow With Love' with marker.

Tote

Sand tote and seal with acrylic spray. Trace and transfer pattern. Paint Light Blue and Dark Green referring to photo. Write 'Friendship Is Like A Garden, Both Need Warmth And Nurturing' with marker.

Cross bars - Cut ends off 12 craft sticks leaving a 4" piece for crossbars. Sand ends and paint Cream. Glue 2 rows of 3 crossbars across front and back of tote. Cut ends off 8 craft sticks leaving 3½". Glue 2 rows of 2 cross bars across each end of tote. Measure down 1¾" from ends of remaining sticks, cut thirty round end pickets. Sand ends, paint Cream. Glue 10 pickets across front and back and 5 across each end of tote.

Flowers - Paint craft picks Bright Green. Cut 48 leaves and 24 stems of varying lengths. Touch up cut ends with paint. Referring to photo, glue stems and leaves on tote. Glue buttons to stems.

Finish - Spray tote with sealer. Place flower pot in one end and gloves across front of tote. Wedge floral foam against pot and gloves to hold them in place. Press fork in foam at back of box. Wedge foam around spade. Cover foam with moss. Glue floral pick to back of seed packet, insert picks in foam. Tie raffia bow on handle near flowers.

And Nurturing

Watering Can Bunny
PHOTO ON PAGE 32
by Jean Kievlan
MATERIALS:
3½" watering can
Tea-dyed 4" stuffed muslin bunny
6" of ⅛" Blue satin ribbon, ⅜" button
Small bunch of silk spring flowers
3" cube of floral foam
Acrylic paint (White, Blue, Orange, Brown, Green, Black)
Acrylic spray finish
Hot glue
Red fine tip permanent marker
INSTRUCTIONS:

Watering Can - Spray can with 2 light coats of finish. Paint sign White and frame Blue. Paint carrots Orange and tops Green. Shade and outline carrots with Brown. Make 'stitches' around sign with Black. Write saying with Red marker. Let paint dry then spray with 2 light coats of finish.

Trim - Wedge floral foam in can. Insert flower stems into foam. Tie ribbon bow and glue to bunny's neck. Glue button in center of bow. Glue bunny on side of can near the handle.

Back Massager
PHOTO ON PAGE 32
by Todd Stiles
MATERIALS:
One 1¾" and two 1¼" wood ball knobs
Two ¾" wood beads
¼" dowel (two 3" and two 2¾" pieces)
Drill and ¼" bit
Wood glue
Red and Black fine-tip permanent markers

INSTRUCTIONS:

Drill 4 holes in bottom of large ball knob. Drill half way through smaller ball knobs and beads to enlarge holes to ¼". Place a small amount of glue in each hole, insert shorter pieces of dowel in front and longer pieces in back holes of large ball knob. Glue ball knobs on ends of longer and beads on ends of shorter dowels. Draw eyes and nose with Black and mouth with Red marker.

ATTACH LEGS TO BOTTOM OF LARGE BALL

Fabric Plant Poke
PHOTO ON PAGE 33
MATERIALS:
6" x 9" of Black/Tan check fabric
3½" x 4½" piece of muslin
2½" x 3½" piece of Blue plaid fabric
HeatnBond™
3 assorted ½" buttons
8" of Gold embroidery floss
Black fabric marker
Pinking shears
Household iron
8" of ⅛" dowel
INSTRUCTIONS:

1. Cut 3" x 4" piece of muslin using pinking shears. Tear two 4" x 5" pieces of check fabric. Following manufacturer's instructions, iron HeatnBond to wrong side of muslin, plaid and one piece of check. Trace and transfer heart pattern to paper side of HeatnBond, cut out heart. Remove paper backing. Place wrong sides of check pieces together, center muslin on check and heart on muslin. Insert end of dowel under muslin. Iron to bond.
2. Make lettering and stitch marks with marker. Thread floss through buttons. Glue floss and buttons to plant poke.

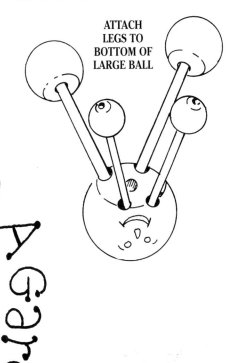

Friends Grow in A Garden

friendship

Seeds

Sunflower in Pot

PHOTO ON PAGE 33

MATERIALS:

3" clay pot
3" cube of floral foam
Spanish moss
Silk sunflower stem with large and small
    flower
1¼" wood circle
Brown yarn
Dark Green and Yellow acrylic paint
Orange paint writer
Small paintbrush
Cosmetic blush
Black fine-tip permanent marker
Hot glue

INSTRUCTIONS:

For face, paint wood circle Yellow. Draw eyes, mouth and freckles with marker. Rub blush on cheeks. Glue face to center of large sunflower. Glue yarn around face. Tie a small yarn bow. Glue bow at top of face. Paint pot Dark Green. Letter 'You Are My Sunshine' with Orange paint writer. Trim foam and wedge into pot. Glue moss to cover top of foam. Insert flower stem into foam.

'Friends Gather Here' Sign

PHOTO ON PAGE 34

*by Shirley Baer, Dianna Koller, Denise
    Basinger*

MATERIALS:

12" and two 2" pieces of 19 gauge wire
½" x 8" piece of Green check fabric
Paintbrushes
Clear acrylic spray sealer
Craft drill
Tacky glue

WOODWORKS WOOD PARTS:

1¼" x 2⅞" x ⁵⁄₁₆" jagged sign
1¹¹⁄₁₆" x 2⁵⁄₁₆" x ¼" country heart
¹⁵⁄₁₆" x 1¹³⁄₁₆" x ³⁄₁₆" bird
1¼" x 1¼" x ³⁄₁₆" sunflower

FOLK ART PAINTS:

Taffy
Nutmeg
Licorice
Bluebonnet
Harvest Gold
Lemon Custard

Coffee Bean
Thicket
Poetry Green
Purple
Primrose

INSTRUCTIONS:

Drill 2 holes in top of sign 2" apart, 2 holes in bottom of sign 1¼" apart and 2 holes in top of heart 1¼" apart.

PAINT:

Sign, heart - Taffy, shade edges Nutmeg.
Bird - Bluebonnet
Sunflower, bird beak - Harvest Gold
Outline beak with Licorice
Sunflower center, petals - Nutmeg, highlight center Coffee Bean, dot - Taffy
Wings - Taffy.
Eye - dot Taffy, add small Licorice dot
Heart, sign - dab lightly with Thicket, Poetry Green, Primrose, Lemon Custard and Purple
Center of Lemon Custard flowers - dot Purple
Leaves - Thicket
Lettering - Licorice

ASSEMBLE:

Curl 12" wire around brush handle, insert ends in top of sign and twist to secure. Attach heart to sign with 2" pieces of wire. Glue bird and sunflower on sign.

FINISH:

Spatter lightly with Licorice. Tie fabric bow around hanger. Spray with sealer.

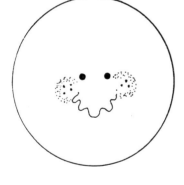

*Friendship is the golden thread that
ties the hands and hearts of all the world.*

Birdhouse Pin

PHOTO ON PAGE 34
by Cindy Bush Cambier

MATERIALS:
Scupley III Clay (Red, Blue, Yellow)
Tac pin and clutch
Rubbing alcohol
Lint-free cloth
Epoxy 220
Wax paper to cover work surface
Single-edge razor blade
Large needle

INSTRUCTIONS:

House - Flatten 1" ball of Blue clay on work surface to 1/8" thick. Using pattern and razor blade, cut out birdhouse. Using needle, pierce hole for door and enlarge by rotating needle inside hole. Smooth edges with your fingers.

Roof - Roll a 2" long Red clay snake 3/16" thick with a thinner center and fatter ends. Press securely onto top of birdhouse pushing ends into shape as shown in photo.

Bird - Starting with a 1/4" Red clay ball, shape into teardrop, flatten and shape bird's body. Shape a smaller Red teardrop, flatten and press onto body for wing. Add a very small amount of Red clay to Yellow clay and knead to an even Gold color. Press a tiny Gold ball to edge of head for beak, then shape into a triangle between 2 fingers. Apply Gold clay dot for eye, pierce center with needle. Add whimsy by applying scattered Gold dots to bird as shown.

Finish - Bake house and bird following clay manufacturer's instructions. Glue bird on birdhouse, let dry. Clean tac pin with alcohol on a lint-free cloth. Glue pin on center back of birdhouse near the top.

**BIRDHOUSE
PATTERN**

**DECORATION
DETAIL**

Floral Cake

PHOTO ON PAGE 35
by Indrani Hawkins

MATERIALS:
3" x 9" styrofoam circle
Green sheet moss
Bird seed
Dried hydrangea
Silk lilacs
14 White freeze dried roses
8 large dried Pink roses
Green galox leaves
1 package of floral pins
Tacky glue
Stiff paintbrush

INSTRUCTIONS:

1. Divide styrofoam into eighths and cut one wedge shaped section from circle. Brush glue around sides on tops of styrofoam pieces. Press moss on glue and secure with floral pins.
2. For cake filling, draw a line of glue around center of cake and cake slice. Press bird seed in glue.
3. Glue leaves around bottom of cake referring to photo. Arrange flowers and leaves on top of cake. Glue, working from edge to center. Glue leaves and flowers on slice to match top of cake.

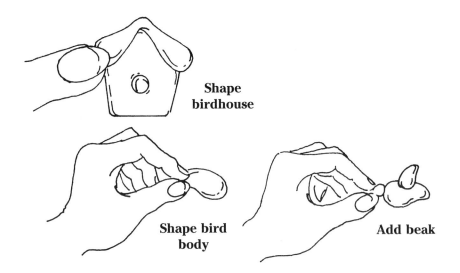

**Shape
birdhouse**

**Shape bird
body**

Add beak

*The language
of friendship is
not words but
sentiments of the
heart and soul.*

Friendship Is Where The ♥ Is

Love Begins At Home

...ins At Home

Friendship Is Where The ♥ Is

*M*y friend Dianne is always a cheerful person. Her favorite expression is, "hold on to that good thought." Because she was blue about moving out of state, I made a frame with friendship sayings to hold all the fond memories and good thoughts that represent our friendship.

Delores Frantz

Friends make life worth living.

My sister Connie and I have an irreplaceable friendship. We have a wild and wacky relationship, but a solid one built on love and devotion. She has a caring heart and shares it generously. I can always count on her for support. I made this flower picture to show her I treasure our friendship.

Becca Cooper

Friends love
at all times.

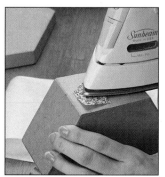

While I'll never be able to repay my mom (left) for everything she has done for me all of my life, I hope the "patchwork heart" I made will serve as a reminder that she is greatly loved. One might say that the various pieces of cloth and decorations that form the heart could symbolize the many lives that she has touched and continues to touch in a positive way throughout her life. If you know some-one with "a heart as big as Texas", this homemade "patchwork heart" gift is the perfect expression of affection.

Donna Tucker

Janet McGowan (right) always encouraged me to be creative. We attended nursing school together in England 15 years ago. Now I live in the United States. Despite the fact that she lives on the other side of the Atlantic, we have remained close friends. This candle is to keep the flame of our friendship glowing.

Carole Turner Eagon

My youngest sister Kelly and I have always had a very special relationship and never lived very far away from one another. Then my husband accepted a new job in another state. A few years and many phone calls later, Kelly confessed that she really missed having her big sister around to look out for her. I gave her a good pep talk and promptly sent this "Big Sister" Guardian Angel that she could carry around in her pocket. Now I am always there for her wherever she goes.

Sandi Egan

No matter where you roam, there is no place quite like home.

Karen Booy has her own pattern company, 'Ewe and Me' and designed a delightful ribbon angel ornament to give to friends she holds most dear. Some like to display their angels all year long.

Karen Booy

When Trey and Liz McNeill, announced they were expecting their second child, friends each decorated one-of-a-kind quilt squares. Stitched together they became a beautiful "Quilt of Love". I just couldn't resist making a companion pillow for their precious gift from God.

Suzanne McNeill

Love Begins At Home

Friendship Is Where The ♡ Is

Farm Scene and Frame

PHOTO ON PAGE 40

by Delores Frantz

MATERIALS:

5" x 7" frame
5" x 7" of cardboard
Assorted fabric scraps
HeatnBond™
Red acrylic paint
Black fine-tip permanent marker
Clear acrylic spray

INSTRUCTIONS:

Transfer patterns to paper side of HeatnBond grouping pieces by fabric color. Allow ⅛" seam allowance where a piece tucks under another piece. Following manufacturer's instructions, bond each group of patterns to wrong side of fabric. Cut out shapes and remove paper backing.

Bond pieces to cardboard in this order: 1-sky, 2-sun, 3-clouds, 4-field, 5-hill, 6-yard, 7-fence, 8-Blue house, 9-path, 10-porch, 11-chimney, 12-roof, 13-posts, 14-porch roof, 15-Red barn, 16-barn roof. Bond remaining shapes in any order. To make the clothesline, glue thread between the trees. Place scene in frame.

Seal frame with Clear acrylic spray. Using Black marker write 'Friendship is where the ♡ Is' across top and bottom and 'Love Begins at Home' on the sides of the frame. Paint hearts Red.

'Best Friends' Bears

PHOTO ON PAGES 40-41

MATERIALS:

Two 6" jointed bears
4" straw hat
5" of ⅛" dowel
2" wood heart
Red acrylic paint
12" of Gold 20 gauge wire
6" of 4mm pearls-by-the-yard
18" of ¼" Blue picot ribbon
9" of ⅜" Red dot ribbon
3 small Blue flowers

Black fine-tip permanent marker
Hot glue

INSTRUCTIONS:

First Bear - Following diagram, bend wire into eye glasses. Press ends of ear pieces through bear's ears. Bend wire down behind each ear to secure. Tie a bow with Red ribbon. Glue bow on one side of bear's head. Drape pearls around neck and secure with glue at the back.

Second Bear - Glue Blue ribbon around hat to make hat band. Cut remaining Blue ribbon in half. Fold end of one piece under ¼" and glue to one side of hat band. Repeat with second piece of ribbon. Glue hat on bear. Fold side of hat down slightly. Tie ribbon under bear's chin and secure with a dot of glue. Glue 3 flowers near one ear.

Glue bears together side by side. Paint heart Red. Write 'Best Friends' on heart with marker. Glue dowel to back of heart and across first bear's arm.

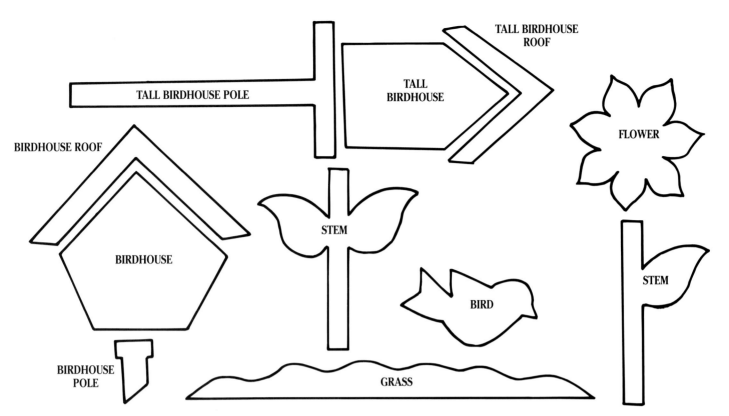

Patterns labeled: TALL BIRDHOUSE POLE, TALL BIRDHOUSE, TALL BIRDHOUSE ROOF, FLOWER, BIRDHOUSE ROOF, BIRDHOUSE, STEM, BIRD, STEM, BIRDHOUSE POLE, GRASS

Birdhouses Memory Box

PHOTO ON PAGE 42

by Delores Frantz

MATERIALS:

10" papier maché 6 sided box
Scraps of cotton print fabrics
HeatnBond™
Tracing and transfer paper
Natural raffia
Black fine tip permanent marker
6 Brown ¾", 6 Burgundy ½" buttons
Household iron, Lo-temp hot glue

INSTRUCTIONS:

Trace each section of appliques separately. Add ⅛" seam allowance to edges that tuck under other pieces. Transfer patterns to paper side of HeatnBond. Place HeatnBond on wrong side of fabric following manufacturer's instructions and iron to fuse. Cut out appliques. Peel off paper backing. Referring to photo, arrange appliques and fuse to box.

Glue ¾" buttons to flowers and ½" button on bird houses. Draw stitch marks around appliques with marker. Write 'The Best Memories Are Shared by Friends' around lid top and 'Memories …Memories' around side of lid. Tie a multi loop raffia bow and glue on lid.

A friend is a found treasure

Pressed Flower Picture

PHOTO ON PAGE 43

MATERIALS:

Pressed flowers and leaves
10" square wood frame with 6" opening
6" square of glass
6" squares of poster board and cardboard
Natural raffia
Black fine-tip permanent marker
1⅛" square sponge
Country Green acrylic paint
Matte Clear acrylic spray finish
White glue

INSTRUCTIONS:

Arrange and glue flowers and leaves on poster board. Write 'A friend is a found treasure' under flowers with Black marker. Seal frame with acrylic finish. Sponge checkerboard pattern on frame with Green paint. Seal with 2 light coats of finish. Place glass and then flower arrangement in frame. Back with cardboard. Tie a raffia bow with long tails. Glue bow at center top of frame. Arrange and glue tails as shown.

Candle with Gold

PHOTO ON PAGE 43

by Carole Turner Eagon

MATERIALS:

Off White pillar candle
Label (from wine or jar)
Plaid Royal Coat
Glamour Dust
Sponge brush
18" of Gold rick rack
GOOP Glue

INSTRUCTIONS:

Paint back of label with Royal Coat. Press label on candle smoothing out wrinkles with your fingers. Paint over whole surface of candle with Royal Coat. While still wet, sprinkle with Glamour Dust. Glue Gold rick rack around top and bottom of candle.

The Best Memories Are Shared by Friends...Memories

Framed Patchwork Heart

PHOTO ON PAGE 43

by Donna Tucker

MATERIALS:

8" x 10" frame
8" x 10" of cardboard
13" x 15" Beige dot fabric
Scraps of assorted Pink, Mauve, Teal and Beige print fabrics
24" of 2.5mm pearls-by-the-yard
24" of 1/2" Ivory gathered lace
Assorted 1/16" to 1/4" Mauve, Ivory, Tan and Teal ribbons
Assorted 1/2" to 1" Ivory lace edgings
Assorted 2mm to 4mm Ivory pearls
3 Ivory 3/8" pearls buttons
3 Ivory 1" crocheted flowers
Pink ribbon rose
4 assorted Brass charms
Polyester fiberfill
HeatnBond™
Black fabric marker
Thick White glue
Hot glue

INSTRUCTIONS:

Trace and transfer patterns to paper side of HeatnBond. Separate patterns and bond to wrong side of fabric scraps. Cut out pieces and remove paper backing. Arrange fabric pieces in center of Beige/Ivory dot fabric.

Use White glue to attach ribbon and lace edgings. Use hot glue to attach charms, pearls and buttons. Starting at center top of heart, hot glue gathered lace and pearls around edge of heart. With marker write 'A Good Friend is a Found Treasure' around edges of heart.

Place fiberfill over cardboard and spread out evenly. Center heart on top of fiberfill. Pull fabric to back and tape. Adjust fabric and add or subtract fiberfill as needed. Remove tape a little at a time and hot glue fabric to back of cardboard as you go. Place heart in frame.

Pocket Angel

PHOTO ON PAGE 44

by Sandi Egan

MATERIALS:

Small flat rock with rounded edges
Acrylic paint:
  White
  Metallic Gold
  Flesh
  White Pearl
  Pink
  Dark Pink
  Light Blue or Light Green
Small paintbrush
Cosmetic Blush
Clear acrylic spray sealer
Black fine-tip permanent marker

INSTRUCTIONS:

Wash and scrub rock with detergent and a stiff brush, let dry. Basecoat rock White. Trace and transfer design, paint.
Face and hands - Flesh.
Eyes - Light Blue. Add White dot highlights.
Cheeks - Pink.
Nose, mouth, eye outlines - Black marker.
Gown - outline Gold.
Halo, wings - Gold, add White Pearl dots.
Necklace - Gold and White Pearl dots.
Cross - Metallic Gold.
Let dry then spray with sealer.

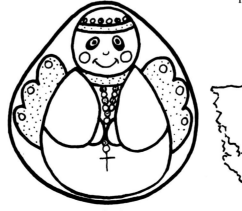

Ribbon Angel Ornament

PHOTO ON PAGE 44

by Karen Booy

MATERIALS:

24" of 3" Gold mesh ribbon
24" of 2" White/Gold star wire edge ribbon
1" wood ball knob
3/4" wood star painted Gold
Gold decorative wedding band
6" of fine Gold cord
Pink cosmetic blush
Hot glue
Needle and thread
Black fine-tip permanent marker

INSTRUCTIONS:

Dress - Tightly gather one long edge of Gold mesh ribbon. Glue to bottom of ball knob.

Arms - Cut 6" of star ribbon, fold in half lengthwise. Pinch center tightly to gather, glue star on top of gathers. Referring to photo, fold ends toward center and glue to front of dress.

Wings - Tie a bow with remaining ribbon, glue to back of head.

Halo and Hanger - Glue seam of wedding band to back of head. Tie ends of Gold cord in a knot, glue knot to head behind halo.

Finish - Make dot eyes with Black marker. Rub blush on cheeks.

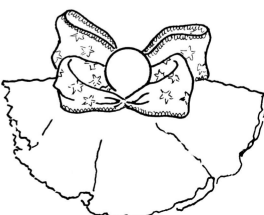

A Baby is a Gift from God.

Friendship Sachet Bags

PHOTO ON PAGE 45
by Helen Rafson

MATERIALS (for each sachet):

6½" wide x 5¾" long piece of print fabric
Matching sewing thread
2" square of solid fabric
    or 2" square of net fabric
12¼" of ¼" coordinating satin ribbon
Potpourri
Fray Check
Small sharp scissors
Pinking shears
Black fine-tip permanent marker or
    water soluble marker
Optional: 6½" of narrow lace edging

INSTRUCTIONS:

For sachet with appliqued heart, trace heart pattern on solid fabric and cut out. Machine applique heart to front of bag. Use the marker to write your friend's name on the heart.

For open heart sachet, trace heart pattern on front of bag with water soluble marker. Center net fabric behind traced heart and machine applique along traced line. Carefully cut fabric from behind net with small scissors.

Fold bag in half and sew a ¼" seam around side and bottom. Trim corners and turn right side out. Trim top of bag with pinking shears or finish with lace edging. Fill bag with potpourri, tie shut with ribbon.

SACHET HEART PATTERN

Quilt or Pillow for Baby

PHOTO ON PAGE 45
by Suzanne McNeill

MATERIALS:

6" squares of flannel:
    Pink, Ivory,
    Pale Gold,
    Blue
3" square of Flesh felt
2 Pink ¾" buttons
Embroidery floss:
    Brown, Pink, Blue,
    Pale Gold, Off White
Two 14" squares of White fabric
1½ yards of 1" Ivory gathered
    lace with Pink ribbon
HeatnBond™
Black fine tip permanent marker
Polyester fiberfill

INSTRUCTIONS:

1. Fuse HeatnBond on flannel following manufacturer's instructions. Trace patterns and transfer to paper side of HeatnBond. Cut out. Fuse flannel pieces to one piece of fabric referring to photo. Blanket stitch around edges of pieces with matching colors using 3 strands of floss.

2. Transfer pattern. Embroider letters and numbers with short straight stitches using 6 strands of Brown floss. French knot period and hair with 6 strands of Brown floss. Sew button for faces with 6 strands of Pink floss. Make eyes with marker.

3. With right sides facing, machine stitch lace to top of pillow with a ½" seam allowance. Sew back of pillow to front leaving a 6" opening on bottom, turn right side out. Stuff with fiberfill and sew opening shut. Top stitch pillow close to lace edge.

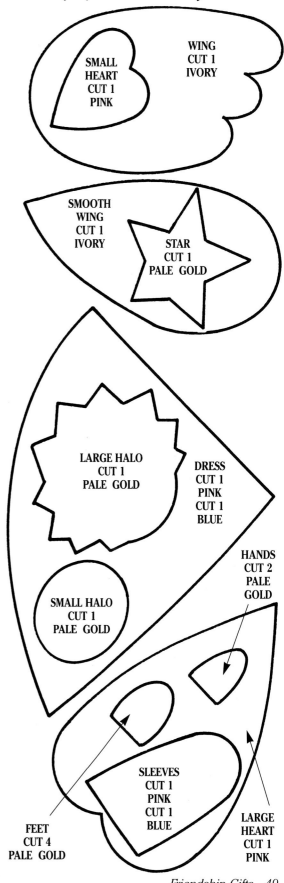

SMALL HEART CUT 1 PINK

WING CUT 1 IVORY

SMOOTH WING CUT 1 IVORY

STAR CUT 1 PALE GOLD

LARGE HALO CUT 1 PALE GOLD

DRESS CUT 1 PINK CUT 1 BLUE

HANDS CUT 2 PALE GOLD

SMALL HALO CUT 1 PALE GOLD

SLEEVES CUT 1 PINK CUT 1 BLUE

FEET CUT 4 PALE GOLD

LARGE HEART CUT 1 PINK

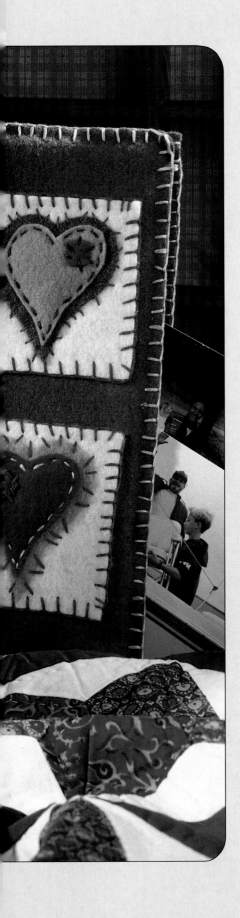

My best friend Elaine Woodring (left) has always been my honorary sister. We were in each other's weddings, helped raise each other's children and have always been there for each other in good times and bad times - just like family.
                                    Jane Sartory

As we share our tears and laughter,
     we'll be friends forever after.

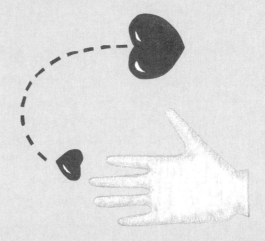

Friendship sings to my soul.

We live 1000 miles apart, but the distance hasn't dampened our friendship nor can it take away the memories of our free-spirited times together.

Maryann Wood O'Kelley (right) is my best friend and the one that introduced me to Country Music and yellow labradors many years ago. Our weekends were spent in the mountains with her guitar, her yellow lab, Lacey, and a Chevy pickup. Maryann is a singer and song writer. The cowboy boots were designed for the truest country girl there is. I had vowed never to place these boots in a craft book because they belonged to Maryann. But this friendship book will truly show how much I LOVE MY FRIEND, MARYANNN.

Kimberly Garringer

The honeymoon hieroglyphic is for my husband and best friend, Jack, in honor of our 15th wedding anniversary. It has been a happy first 15 years and we look forward to our future years together.

Seventeen years ago I would go to work each morning and find a clean drafting table. That wasn't the way I left it. My desk was the only one that was being tidied up at night by this mystery person. Several months went by before I finally met Jack, who was working the night shift at my desk. We were married two years later. He still picks up after me.

Patty Cox

 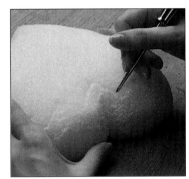 

Friends are always there, everything else comes and goes.

My best friend is Lisa K. McDade (left). She lives in Crossville, Tennessee, near the beautiful mountains. Lisa has a 98 acre farm near her home where we go camping and fishing. On this farm with Lisa's family, I have spent some of the happiest days of my life. Lisa, whose mother is a Native American, loves Native crafts. This friendship necklace was designed especially for Lisa. God blessed me with this wonderful friendship and I am thankful.

Pam Lane

For years my cousin, Tara (left), has been my friend and idol, but we don't see each other too often since she lives in California now. I knew she liked refrigerator magnets that are different so I decided to bead some that would also remind her of me. She was very pleased with the results.

Donna Kennedy

I made this blessing gourd for my niece, Karin Matlack. We have had a special relationship since she was a tiny child… I am her 'other mom'. She and her family are moving. This gift will be a symbol of the many blessings I wish for them in their new home.

Colleen Reigh

Even though we have always lived hundreds of miles apart, my cousin, Vicki, and I have always felt a special bond. At family gatherings we always singled each other out. Our friendship has continued to grow over the years fueled by letters, phone calls and occasional visits. Her love of Native American crafts inspired me to make her a Kachina Doll.

Virginia Tucker

Felt Album Cover

PHOTO ON PAGE 50-51

by Kim Ballor

MATERIALS:

Photo album
Felt (Blue, Antique Ivory, Cranberry, Purple, Green, Antique Gold)
Embroidery floss (Gold, Cranberry, Purple, Green)
3 buttons
Yardstick
Crewel needle

INSTRUCTIONS:

Open photo album. Measure open length and height. Cut a piece of Blue felt for cover that is length + 1" by height + ½". Cut 2 inner pieces 4" by height + ½". Cut a piece of Antique Ivory felt 3" x 9". Cut 2 pieces 3½" x 3½". Blanket stitch in place referring to photo using desired color of floss. Cut 2 large hearts and 5 small hearts from desired colors of felt. Cut 2 small squares of felt for patches. Referring to photo, stitch all pieces in place. Tie buttons to 3 hearts on left side of album. Blanket stitch inner pieces to inside ends of cover. Blanket stitch all the way around the cover.

'Bear Hug' Bear

PHOTO ON PAGE 50

MATERIALS:

12" jointed plush bear
1 yard of 1" Dark Green ribbon
5 assorted buttons
Baby's breath
6" square of thin cotton batting
5" squares of cotton patchwork fabric
4" squares of Ivory cotton fabric
HeatnBond™
Pinking shears
Black fabric marker
Ivory and 2 Burgundy ribbon roses
Hot glue

INSTRUCTIONS:

Glue 7" of ribbon around neck. Fold a 4-loop bow and secure with wire. Glue bow to neck. Glue roses in center of bow. Glue baby's breath around roses. Following manufacturer's instructions, apply HeatnBond to wrong side of patchwork and Ivory fabrics. Transfer large heart pattern to paper side of patchwork fabric and small heart pattern to paper side of Ivory fabric. Cut out hearts with pinking shears. Remove paper backing. Layer batting, large heart and small heart. Bond the 3 layers together. Trim edge of batting with pinking shears leaving ¼" showing. Write 'Friendship is a Bear Hug' on the Ivory heart with the marker, and glue in bear's hands.

Cowboy Boot Earrings

PHOTO ON PAGE 52

by Kimberly Garringer

MATERIALS:

3" stick of Teal Green Friendly Plastic®
3" stick of Silver Cobra Friendly Plastic®
2 Silver fishhook ear wires
Large sewing needle, Home oven
Cookie sheet, Non stick cooking spray

INSTRUCTIONS:

1. Trace pattern. Cut 1 boot from Teal Green and 1 boot top from Silver Cobra. Reverse patterns and repeat to make opposite earring.
2. Coat cookie sheet with non stick spray. Place boots on cookie sheet so that the top pieces slightly overlap the tops of the boots. Bake at 250°F for 4½ minutes. Remove from oven.
3. Etch ankle strapping with needle. Use needle to gently pull Silver Cobra down over the Teal Green 4 times on each boot. Cool.
4. Heat needle point with match and pierce hole in top corner of each boot. Attach ear wires.

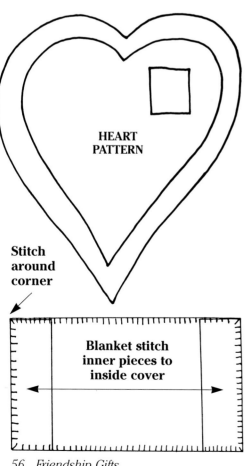

HEART PATTERN

Stitch around corner

Blanket stitch inner pieces to inside cover

Friendship is a Bear Hug

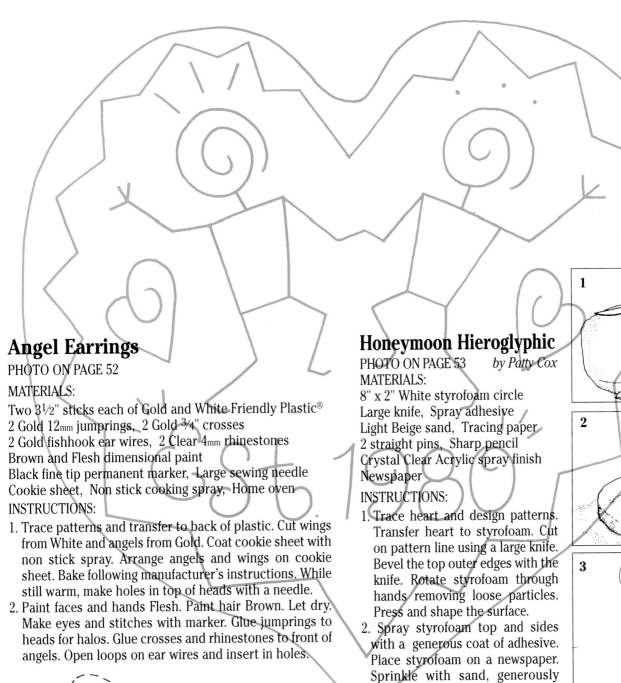

Angel Earrings

PHOTO ON PAGE 52

MATERIALS:

Two 3½" sticks each of Gold and White Friendly Plastic®
2 Gold 12mm jumprings, 2 Gold ¾" crosses
2 Gold fishhook ear wires, 2 Clear 4mm rhinestones
Brown and Flesh dimensional paint
Black fine tip permanent marker, Large sewing needle
Cookie sheet, Non stick cooking spray, Home oven

INSTRUCTIONS:

1. Trace patterns and transfer to back of plastic. Cut wings from White and angels from Gold. Coat cookie sheet with non stick spray. Arrange angels and wings on cookie sheet. Bake following manufacturer's instructions. While still warm, make holes in top of heads with a needle.

2. Paint faces and hands Flesh. Paint hair Brown. Let dry. Make eyes and stitches with marker. Glue jumprings to heads for halos. Glue crosses and rhinestones to front of angels. Open loops on ear wires and insert in holes.

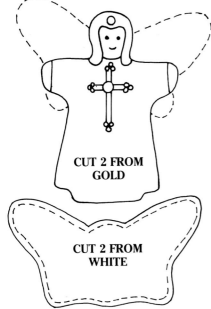

CUT 2 FROM GOLD

CUT 2 FROM WHITE

Honeymoon Hieroglyphic

PHOTO ON PAGE 53   *by Patty Cox*

MATERIALS:

8" x 2" White styrofoam circle
Large knife, Spray adhesive
Light Beige sand, Tracing paper
2 straight pins, Sharp pencil
Crystal Clear Acrylic spray finish
Newspaper

INSTRUCTIONS:

1. Trace heart and design patterns. Transfer heart to styrofoam. Cut on pattern line using a large knife. Bevel the top outer edges with the knife. Rotate styrofoam through hands removing loose particles. Press and shape the surface.

2. Spray styrofoam top and sides with a generous coat of adhesive. Place styrofoam on a newspaper. Sprinkle with sand, generously covering all surfaces. Lift and tap styrofoam to remove excess sand.

3. Apply a second coat of spray adhesive. Sprinkle generously with sand. Lift and tap to remove excess sand. Lift sand-filled newspaper and fold at center. Return excess sand to bag.

4. Spray stone with a generous coat of sealer. Let dry a few minutes.

5. Center design pattern on stone, secure with straight pins. Using the lead of a sharpened pencil, puncture tracing and surface of heart with a series of dots. Remove paper. Run pencil lead over tracing breaking apart dots and deepening the design.

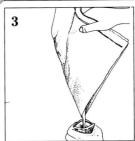

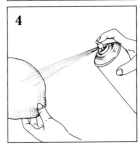

Squash Blossom Beaded Necklace

PHOTO ON PAGE 53

MATERIALS:

12" x 18" piece of White pigskin
Size 10 Gunmetal seed beads
Size 11 Opaque Turquoise seed beads
Beading thread and needles

INSTRUCTIONS:

Beaded Pieces - Trace shapes for necklace pieces. Transfer to pigskin leaving 2" between each shape. Couch beads on pigskin following beading technique diagram and referring to photo. Cut out pieces close to beading. Cut matching pieces to back each piece.

Assemble Medallion - Stitch backing to bottom left piece of medallion following Edge Beading Diagram. Stitch backing to second piece, attaching second piece to first piece referring to Medallion 'Attaching Medallion Pieces' Diagram. Continue adding medallion pieces as shown. Hide knots and tails between beading and backing pieces.

Necklace - Stitch backing to necklace pieces. Following Daisy Chain Diagram, attach necklace pieces and medallion using 2 rows of Daisy Chain with 5 pattern repeats on inside row and 6 repeats on outside row. Add 2 rows to top of last necklace pieces.

Back of Necklace - Join 2 rows of Daisy Chain at end of necklace following the 'End of Chain' Diagram. Make 9" of Daisy Chain, attach to ends rows on opposite side of necklace. Tie off and run ends back through several pattern repeats.

Squash Blossoms - Referring to photo, bead squash blossoms following Squash Blossom Diagram. Hide knots and tails between beading and backing pieces.

BEADING TECHNIQUES

Outlining. Sew 4 beads down along outline of the design. Return needle back to top by passing the needle and thread through center line of beads and out through last 2 beads. Add 4 more beads. Change color of beads following color pattern of the design. If the area is too small for 4 beads, add 1 bead at a time until area is filled. Or sew 1 bead at a time. Thread a bead on needle, take small stitch and come out of pigskin just in front of bead.

Filling Design Area. After outlining, bead next row following curve of design or arrows on pattern. The rows of beads are not spiraled, each row is complete in itself. Repeat until area is filled

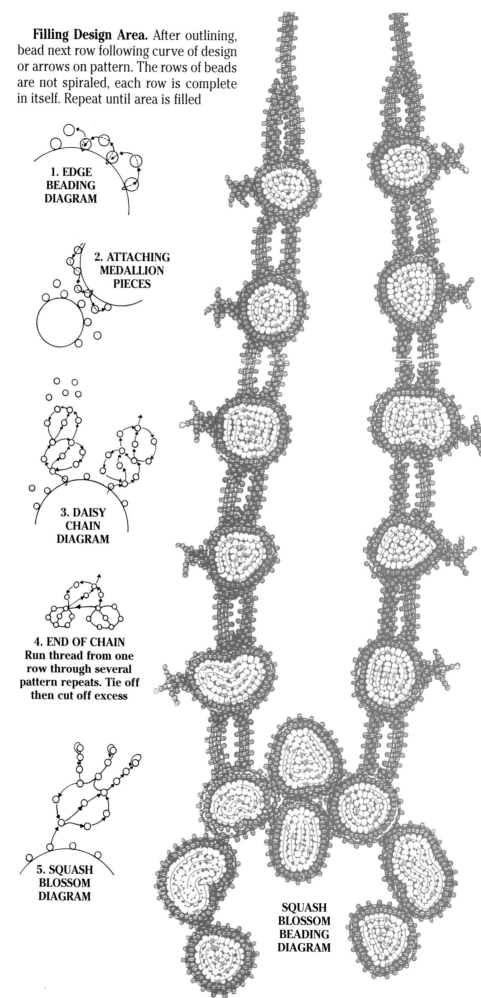

1. EDGE BEADING DIAGRAM

2. ATTACHING MEDALLION PIECES

3. DAISY CHAIN DIAGRAM

4. END OF CHAIN
Run thread from one row through several pattern repeats. Tie off then cut off excess

5. SQUASH BLOSSOM DIAGRAM

SQUASH BLOSSOM BEADING DIAGRAM

**HEART
CUT 2
BLACK FELT**

*A true friend
is a companion
of the heart.*

Native American Friendship Necklace

PHOTO ON PAGE 54
by Pam Lane

MATERIALS:

4" x 8" piece of Black felt
Size 11 seed beads (Silver, White, Turquoise)
Four size 10/0 Purple seed beads
Beading thread, 2 beading needles
Small amount of fiberfill
Tracing paper, White transfer paper
2 yards of Turquoise rattail

INSTRUCTIONS:

1. Trace pattern. Cut 2 hearts from felt. Transfer beading pattern to one heart.
2. Thread needle, knot end and pass through felt from back to front. String a number of pattern repeats or required number of beads to cover pattern line on felt. Thread second needle and bring up near the start of beads. Bring needle up after first 3 beads. Sew over thread between beads 3 and 4. Push beads together and repeat bringing needle up between beads 6 and 7. Couch between groups of 3 beads to maintain pattern shape.
3. Sew felt hearts together leaving a small opening, stuff with fiberfill and sew opening closed. Sew sets of 3 Silver beads diagonally around edge of heart.
4. Attach 4 bead loops to bottom back of heart. String beads for each loop as follows: 20 White, 5 Turquoise, 3 Silver, 1 Purple, reverse and repeat pattern from Silver beads.
5. Cut rattail in half. Fold each piece in half and sew the folds to top back sides of heart. Tie knots in rattail close to folds and 4" from folds. Tie ends of rattail together.

COUCH BEADS
Form tiny stitches over thread in strung beads.

SEW FOLDS TO SIDES ON BACK OF HEART.

BEADING PATTERN

Loom Beaded Magnets

PHOTO ON PAGE 54
by Donna Kennedy

MATERIALS:

Beading loom
Beading thread, needle
GOOP glue
1/2" or 1" round magnets
Buffalo: Seed beads (White, Turquoise, Black)
    1" x 2" piece of Turquoise suede
Man: Seed beads (Turquoise, Red, White, Black, Orange, Brown)
    1" x 2" piece of Turquoise suede
Blanket: Seed beads (Red, Blue, Turquoise)
    1" x 2" pieces of Grey suede
Tepee: Seed beads (Turquoise, Orange, Yellow, Black)
    1" x 1¼" piece of Grey suede

INSTRUCTIONS:

1. Thread loom with warp threads following manufacturer's instructions. Count the beads in the width of the design to determine the number of warp threads. One more warp thread than the number of beads is required.
2. Use beading needle and thread for weft. Tie the first bead of the design to the end of the thread. Add remaining beads for the first row. Place beads under warp threads, press beads up between warp threads with

continued on page 60

Loom Beaded Magnets

continued from page 59

finger. Pass weft thread around end of warp thread and back through each bead with weft thread on top of warp threads. Repeat for remaining rows of beads.

3. At the ends of the design, run the needle back though several rows of beads. Trim thread near the edge of the final bead. Remove beaded piece from loom. Tie warp thread together and fold to back of design, tape in place. Glue beadwork to front and magnet to back of suede.

Note - To add weft thread, tie tails of original thread and new thread to a warp thread at the end of a row. Run each tail through 5 or 6 beads, trim close to a bead.

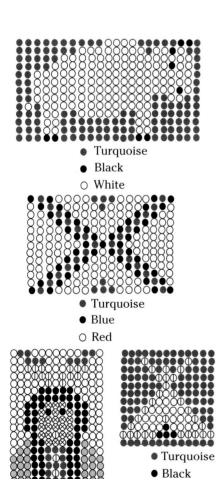

• Turquoise
• Black
○ White

• Turquoise
• Blue
○ Red

• Turquoise ◍ Red
• Black ◔ Brown
○ White ⊗ Orange

• Turquoise
• Black
◍ Red
○ Yellow

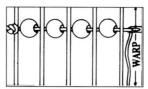

Loom. String warp threads on the loom according to manufacturer's instructions. Count beads in width of design to determine number of warp threads. You will need one more warp thread than the number of beads.

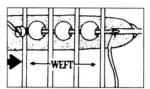

Needle. Use beading needle and thread for weft. Tie first bead of design to end of thread. Add remaining beads for first row. Lay beads BENEATH warp threads and press them up between warp threads with left finger.

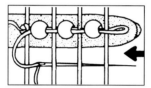

Take the Thread around the end warp thread and pass it back through each bead with needle, this time running needle on TOP of the warp threads. Pull thread tight. Next, string the 2nd row of beads, repeating as before.

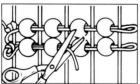

New Thread. To add a new thread: at the end of a piece of thread, tie the tail to a warp thread at the end of a row. Place a dot of glue on the knot to secure it. Run each tail back through 5 or 6 beads. Finally, cut the tail off close to a bead.

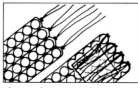

Finish Work. At the end of design, run needle back through several rows of beads. Trim thread near edge of final bead. Remove from loom. Tie off warp threads. Fold warp threads to back of design. Hold in place with tape.

House Blessing Gourd

PHOTO ON PAGE 55
by Colleen Reigh

MATERIALS:
5" natural gourd
1¼" Silver eye pin
Two 4mm Silver beads
6mm Amber bead
6mm Silver jumpring
3 Silver feather charms
40" of Tan shoelace leather strip
Assorted stones, Large needle
Artificial sinew, Craft knife
Round nose pliers, Wire cutters
Acrylic spray finish

INSTRUCTIONS:

Gourd - Using a craft knife, carefully cut top off gourd with a slightly wavy line. Remove seeds and pulp. Spray gourd with 2 light coats of finish. Thread needle with sinew. Beginning at center front and leaving 2" free, couch one leather strip around opening ⅜" from edge. Overlap ends. Couch second strip next to first alternating stitch placement.

Trim - Referring to photo, thread beads on eye pin. Trim straight end of eye pin to ⅜" and bend into a loop with pliers. Open jumpring and thread on feathers with largest in the center. Attach jumpring to top of eye pin. Sew around overlapped ends of leather several times catching top of eye pin in stitches.

Place stones in gourd.

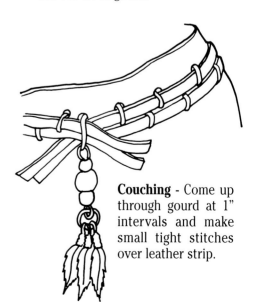

Couching - Come up through gourd at 1" intervals and make small tight stitches over leather strip.

House Blessing Gourd

The stones in a House Blessing Gourd are said to provide protection against harmful influences. Personalize each gourd by adding stones to suit the needs of the recipient.

Agate - danger

Amber - illness

Adventurine - bad luck

Bone - bad feelings

Barite Rose - lack of energy

Carnelian - inaction

Chalcedony - past trauma

Jasper - fears and guilt

Garnet - insecurity and money loss

Lapis Lazuli - bad judgement

Malachite - undesirable business associations

Moonstone - dangers while traveling

Obsidian - emotional draining by others

Opal - lack of love and romance

Pearl - unbalanced love

Peridot - depression

Quartz - self blocks

Rhodonite - lack of self esteem

Shell - lack of organization

Sodalite - lack of inner peace

Tigereye - bad decisions and impulsiveness

Turquoise - worrisome people

OPEN AND ATTACH JUMPRING

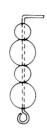

THREAD BEADS ON EYE PIN

Corn Kachina Doll

PHOTO ON PAGE 55

by Virginia Tucker

MATERIALS:

4 ears of mini Indian corn with husks
Large acorn with cap
18" of floral wire
GOOP glue

INSTRUCTIONS:

1. Soak husk ends of corn in warm water for 10 minutes or until husks become soft. Place 2 ears of corn side by side and divide husks into 3 equal sections. Braid husks for 4". Add husks from remaining ears and continue to braid stopping 3" from end of husks. Let dry. Cut wire in half. Wrap one piece of wire tightly around end of braid.

2. Wrap remaining wire around stem of acorn. Glue wire to acorn stem. Let dry and trim stem. Wrap this wire twice around the end of braid to secure acorn head. Make a hanging loop with end of wire and twist to tighten.

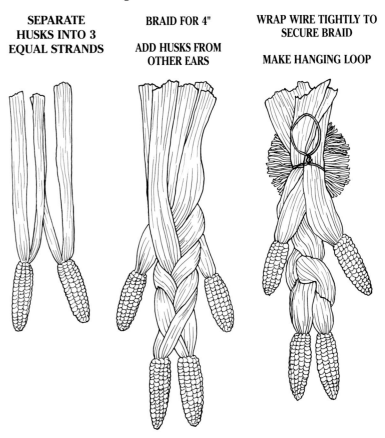

SEPARATE HUSKS INTO 3 EQUAL STRANDS

BRAID FOR 4"

ADD HUSKS FROM OTHER EARS

WRAP WIRE TIGHTLY TO SECURE BRAID

MAKE HANGING LOOP

Friendship is a special safe place which lives within one's heart.

*M*y 'Uncle Bill' is always doing something nice for me. Once when I was stranded because of car problems, he came to my rescue. As a thank-you for his continued kindness, I always make sure his special cookie box is full of his favorite chocolate chip cookies.

Laura Kievlan

Friendship is the golden thread that binds hearts together.

On hot summer days, my friend Janet Teague (right) and I loved to talk and drink cold Dr. Peppers. When she moved to Alaska, we missed having our visits and our Dr. Peppers. One day I asked her if she had one wish what would it be. Her reply...that we could just sit together and drink cold Dr. Peppers. This gift was the closest we could be.

Debby Quillin

Joanne (right) and I became friends through our children. We talk just about every day, babysit for one another and have been known to spend long summer nights sitting on the porch talking. Our friendship has grown from a quiet "hello" to a 'noisy chatter' just like the Bell Bunny - a quiet looking bunny ringing out with the sound of friendship.

Deborah Scheblein

Friends Forever

My best friend, Janice Sherman (right), is very much into recycling. So this used tuna can scrubby holder is the perfect gift for her. It's true. "I would scour the world for a friend like her!"

Phyllis Sandford

My dynamic friend, Marilyn Carroll (right), who is always full of ideas and laughter, redecorated her kitchen with daisies and hearts. Since we both love crafts and crafting, I stitched her a handmade gift towel to fit into her new decor.

Liz Lusk

Judy Huxford (left) and I have known each other since the first grade. Some of our wild and crazy memories include antics, like calling people anonymously at midnight on New Year's Eve and playing "Auld Lang Syne." Judy and I long ago gave up childhood pranks for families and jobs, but no matter how busy we are, we never miss spending a New Year's Eve together!

Carol Krob

For over twenty years Margaret Curley (left) and I have traveled with our team to National Bowling Conventions. Just before the 1987 convention, I received some bad news. The night of the convention banquet, it all caught up with me and I was too distraught to attend. Margaret stayed behind to comfort me while the others went ahead. That night I realized she was a caring and unselfish friend.

Gin Rich

My mother Margaret and I are best friends. We like to do lots of things together...go shopping, see movies, eat at our favorite salad bar, attend stage productions and travel. Once we took off with my two small children for 3 weeks in her big motor home. We had a lot of fun. Upon our return we realized how brave we had been. We had fearlessly headed down the highway with less than 25 miles of 'Big Red' driving experience between us.

Barbara Burnett

friends bring such happiness.

My special friend, Margaret Hanson (left), seems to go non-stop. At one point, she had three jobs, plus a family! Even so, she still found time for me. When my son died, she helped me fill the large hole left in my heart. My friendship gift to her is a reminder to take some time for herself.

Judy McKinney

CHOCOLATE CHIP COOKIES

Heart Cookies
PHOTO ON PAGE 62
by Virginia Tucker
MATERIALS:
4" clay pot with saucer
4" cube of Green floral foam
Three $\frac{1}{4}$" dowels (8", 9" and 10")
Sugar cookie dough
3" and $3\frac{1}{2}$" heart cookie cutters
Decorator frosting (Red, White, Green)
Frosting piping bag with star and writing decorator tips
Red and Green tissue paper
Red and Gold metallic $\frac{1}{4}$" ribbon
Red/Green $\frac{3}{8}$" grosgrain ribbon
Small sponge, Small paintbrush
GOOP glue
Acrylic paints (Red, Pink, White, Green)
INSTRUCTIONS:
Cookies - Make sugar cookie dough using a favorite recipe. Roll dough $\frac{1}{8}$" thick. Cut out four $3\frac{1}{2}$" and two 3" heart cookies. Place three cookies on baking sheet. Place tip of a dowel in center of each cookie, cover with matching heart, press together. Bake cookies according to recipe until firm but not browned. Remove from oven and let cool.

Pot - Basecoat pot and saucer Dark Red, let dry. Paint saying on one side of pot White. Paint Pink heart under saying. Make sets of 3 Pink dots around rim of pot. Cut heart shape from sponge. Dip sponge in White and Pink paint, sponge hearts randomly on pot, let dry. Add Green stems with paintbrush. Glue pot in center of saucer. Glue Red/Green ribbon around rim of saucer. Make a Red/Green bow and glue to front of pot.

Finish - Trim floral foam to fit in pot. Cut a piece of each color tissue paper to line pot as shown. Push foam firmly into pot. Alternating Pink and White, pipe frosting stars around edges of cookies on front and back. Write words on cookie with Green frosting. Insert dowels into foam. Tie metallic ribbon around each dowel, curl ends.

Red tissue

Green tissue

Floral foam

SPONGE PATTERN

Friendship Comes From The ♡

Friends Are Hugs For The Heart

In the Cookie of Life, Friends are the Chocolate Chips.

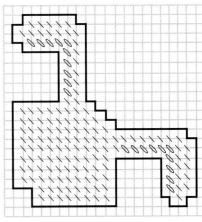

BUNNY HEAD FRONT

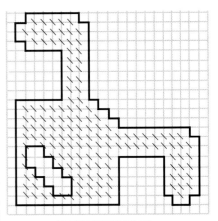

BUNNY HEAD BACK

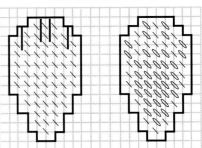

BACK FEET - WORK 2 OF EACH

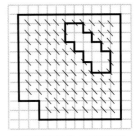

BUNNY HEAD BOTTOM

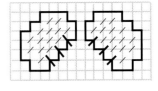

FRONT FEET

GREY   WHITE   PINK

Cookie Box

PHOTO ON PAGES 62-63
by Laura Kievlan
MATERIALS:
Round papier maché box
Acrylic paint
 (Off White, Red, Dark Brown, Tan)
Small round and flat paintbrushes
Small sponge
INSTRUCTIONS:
 Basecoat lid Off White. Basecoat outside of box Red. Sponge Tan spots on lid.
 Add chocolate chips with Dark Brown and highlight with Off White. Paint saying on lid Black and words on side of box Off White.

Dr. Pepper Rabbit

PHOTO ON PAGE 64
by Debby Quillin
MATERIALS:
Unopened Dr. Pepper can, Plush rabbit
Individually wrapped candy
18" of White 1" beading lace
18" of Burgundy 1/16" satin ribbon
White curly ribbon, Hot glue
2 flexible plastic drinking straws
INSTRUCTIONS:
 Hot glue candy to cover top of can. Cut straws to 3" and glue near center. Thread the satin ribbon through the lace and wrap around rabbit's head under ears. Tie ends in a bow. Secure headband to rabbit with hot glue. Position rabbit with mouth near the top of one straw. Tie the rabbit to the can with curly ribbon. Ribbon goes around rabbit's waist and just under top rim of can.

Bell Bunny

PHOTO ON PAGE 64
by Deborah Scheblein
MATERIALS:
3" White bell
1 sheet of 7 count plastic canvas
Yarn (Pink, White, Grey)
Two 1/2" movable eyes, Two 1/2" White pompons
1/2" Pink pompon, 2" White pompon
12" piece of 5/8" Pink satin ribbon
INSTRUCTIONS
 Cut and work plastic canvas pieces as indicated by chart. Stitch the front and the back head pieces together leaving the bottom open to attach the bottom piece. Attach the bottom piece to the head pieces. Stitch the front and back of the feet together.
 Glue the head on the top of the bell, inserting the bell hanger through the slit in the plastic canvas. Glue the front feet to the top half of the bell. Glue the back feet to the lower half of the bell. Glue the movable eyes in place. Glue the White pompons for the cheeks and the Pink pompon for the nose in place. Glue the 2" pompon to the back of the bell for the tail. Thread Pink ribbon through the bell hanger, make a hanging loop and knot.

Tuna Can Scrubby Holder

PHOTO ON PAGE 65

by Phyllis Sandford

MATERIALS:

Tuna can, Copper 'scrubby'

Acrylic paint (Ebony Black, Buttermilk, Gooseberry Pink, Olive Green)

DecoArt Satin Varnish

1" sponge brush, Flat sponge

Loew-Cornell series 7350 Liner brush size 0

Stylus large point series S-50

INSTRUCTIONS:

Wash tuna can in dishwasher or in hot soapy water. Rinse with vinegar, let dry. Using 1" sponge brush, sponge several light coats of Buttermilk on tuna can. Let dry completely between coats. Cut flat sponge into ½" square. Dip sponge into Gooseberry Pink, paint checks. Paint 'I've scoured the earth for a friend like you!' using the liner brush dipped into Ebony Black. Using the large end of the stylus, dip into Olive Green and paint dots in between checks. Let paint dry completely. Varnish using the 1" sponge brush. Place scrubby in can.

Friendship Towel

PHOTO PAGE 65

by Liz Lusk

MATERIALS:

Homespun fabric tea towel

½ yard of 1¾" Ecru crochet ruffled lace

1¾ yard of ¼" Yellow satin ribbon

5" x 3" of Blue with Yellow flowers fabric

3 Yellow sunflower buttons

White sewing thread and needle

Fabric glue

INSTRUCTIONS:

Using patterns, cut hearts from fabric. Referring to photo, glue hearts to front center of towel 2" from bottom edge. Blanket stich around edges of hearts. Sew a button at the top of each heart. Glue lace across bottom of towel on back. Glue ribbon across bottom of towel on front. Tie a ribbon bow and glue to center of ribbon.

Blue Paper Angel

PHOTO ON PAGE 66   *by Gin Rich*

MATERIALS:

One 22mm and two 12mm wood beads

5" x 20" piece of Blue wallpaper

12" of Opal mesh stretch ribbon

3 Gold ¾" star charms

5" of Blue rattail cord, 3" of doll hair

9" of ⅛" Burgundy/Gold ribbon

4" of 3mm Ivory pearls-by-the-yard

Peach acrylic paint, Paintbrush

Red & Black fine tip permanent markers

INSTRUCTIONS:

Paint beads Peach. Draw face with markers. Fold wallpaper in half and glue together. Trace and transfer dress and sleeves to wallpaper. Cut out one dress and two sleeves. Shape dress in a cone, overlap edges and glue. Repeat for sleeves. Glue head over tip of large cone. Glue sleeves to side of dress and hands in sleeves.

Glue tip of stars on cord and cord in hand beads. Tie ribbon bow and glue on neck. Fluff and spread hair, glue on head. Glue pearls in circle for halo, glue halo on head.

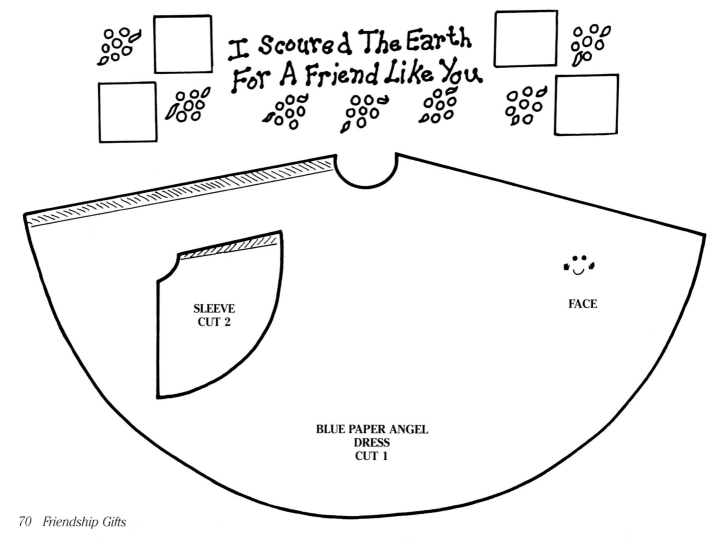

I Scoured The Earth For A Friend Like You

SLEEVE
CUT 2

FACE

BLUE PAPER ANGEL
DRESS
CUT 1

Notes from Judy

PHOTO ON PAGE 66
by Carol Krob

MATERIALS:
Sheet of Light Blue 14-mesh plastic
   canvas, cut as directed
#24 tapestry needle, #10 crewel needle
Light Blue quilting thread
Small Mauve ribbon rose
Plastic canvas cutter
Three 1½" x 2" Post-it™ note pads

COLOR KEY
DMC Embroidery Floss
   /   519   Sky Blue
   /   321   Light Navy Blue
   ♡   3689   Light Mauve
       3685   Dark Mauve
   〇   White
Mill Hill Beads
   ●   358   Cobalt Blue

INSTRUCTIONS:
Cut canvas - one piece 42 holes wide x 54 holes high (front), two squares 23 x 23 holes (sides), two pieces 23 x 30 holes (back and bottom).

Stitch - Thread tapestry needle with floss and stitch design on front following chart. Use half-cross, cross and slanting gobelin stitches. Use letter chart to personalize with your friend's name or initials. Add straight stitches last using Light Navy Blue for eyelids and eyebrows and Dark Mauve for mouth.

Beading - Thread crewel needle with quilting thread. Anchor thread by weaving through stitches on back. Attach beads individually with half-cross stitches (lower left to upper right). Light Navy Blue cross stitches may be substituted for beads.

Cut - Place stitched piece on cutting surface, cut to finished shape following solid heavy outline on chart. Stitch ribbon rose on left side of head.

Assemble - With Light Navy Blue floss, whipstitch front and and side sections to bottom section then whipstitch together to form corners of box. Insert note pads.

Each square on chart = one canvas hole.

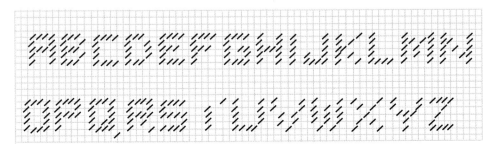

Noah's Ark Bath Basket

PHOTO ON PAGE 67
by Judy McKinney

MATERIALS:
Round White basket with straight sides
Hand towel, Hand soap
Shower and bath gel, Soft mesh sponge
Body lotion, Candle in glass jar
Romance or mystery paperback book
Small box of chocolates
½ yard each of Medium & Dark Blue fabric
Noah's Ark buttons from LaMode
Pinking shears, Small safety pin
Fabric glue or hot glue

INSTRUCTIONS:
Fabric Bands - Measure around basket, rolled hand towel, candle and bar of soap. Multiply total of measurements by 2. Cut 2½" wide strips from each color of fabric. Sew short ends of strips together to equal total measured length. Place wrong sides together, stitch 1⅛" from each long edge to form a casing for the elastic. Measure the length around each item. Cut a band twice the length and cut elastic the same length as each item. Use a safety pin to insert the elastic through the casing. Gather to fit and tie a knot in the elastic. If band slides down basket, secure with hot glue.

Book Cover - Fits book approximately 4⅛" x 6¾" x ¾". Cut 7¼" x 13" rectangles from each color of fabric and batting. Sandwich batting between fabric rectangles and stitch ¼" from each edge. Trim edge with pinking shears. Fold ends 2" to inside, stitch at top and bottom. Slide book cover in folds.

Finish - Cut shanks off buttons and glue in place.

Bubble Vase

PHOTO ON PAGE 67
by Barbara Burnett

MATERIALS:
6" x 9" Clear vase
52 ounces of Ice Blue floral gems
Quick Grab Contact adhesive

INSTRUCTIONS:
Following manufacturer's instructions, glue rows of gems around base of container. Continue gluing gems in a random pattern resembling bubbles floating up. In some places, glue a second and third layer.

*T*his frame was designed with my two little granddaughters in mind. They are 14 months apart. Not only are they sisters, they are Best Friends. If you can't find a frame similar to this one, simply paint the design on a mat board or cut one using a craft knife and balsa wood.

Dorris Sorensen

A friend loves at all times.

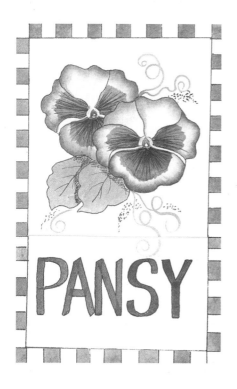

PANSY

My Aunt Juana (left) holds a special place in my heart. She is always willing to share her knowledge with me. For my wedding and in honor of our African-American heritage, she taught me the tradition of 'jumping the brooms' just as the slaves did many years ago. My gift of a family photo tree is a gift to celebrate her warmth and caring.

Tanya Lovejoy

I made these Hershey Kiss® candy rosebuds for my best friend Libby Schmid (left) on the occasion of our 20 year class reunion. The yellow roses signify long lasting friendships, even after long absences.
Marilyn Hargens

Friendship is a special blessing.

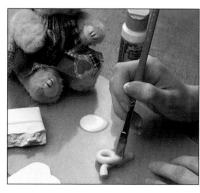

Friends for Life

My baby, Katie, and her cousin Joey are going to grow up to be the best of friends, just as his mother Michele Gagner and I are. This hand-made frame picture is a loving acknowledgement of our friendship.

Etsuko Suzuki

I made this flower pot for my friend Karen Simms (left). She and I have a great deal in common. I will be thinking of her and she will call. We like the same styles and ideas, yet like flowers we are each individuals with very different personalities.

Diane Bliss

In our work together for Design Originals, Barbara Burnett and I frequently attend trade shows and make television appearances. As a memento for Barbara of one of our Tennessee TV taping trips, I handpainted this frame.

Julie McGuffee

Friends are like flowers
in life's garden.

ABCDEFGHIJKLMNOPQRSTUVWXYZ

'Friends' Birdhouse Frame

PHOTO ON PAGE 72
by Dorris Sorensen

MATERIALS:
7½" square wood frame with 2" opening
Miracle sponges
Clear satin spray finish
Paint brushes -
  #4 round, #8 flat, #10 flat, stipple, liner,
Black fine-tip permanent marker
DELTA® CERAMCOAT PAINT COLORS:
  White, Nightfall Blue, Red Iron Oxide, Barn Red, Liberty Blue, Empire Gold, Crocus Yellow, Brown Iron Oxide, Black, Lime Green, Woodland Night Green
Delta® crackle medium

INSTRUCTIONS:
  Basecoat entire frame with 2 coats of Nightfall Blue, let dry between coats. Apply a coat of crackle medium according to directions on the bottle. Apply crackle to front of frame, let dry. Paint front of frame with 1 coat of White to crackle, let dry. Trace and transfer pattern.
  Cut ⅜" square of sponge, dip in Red Iron Oxide. Paint checkerboard design on border of frame. Basecoat birdhouse and chimney Liberty Blue, shade on left side with Nightfall Blue. Shade roof with Brown Iron Oxide. Triple load #10 round brush with Brown Iron Oxide, Black and White, paint birdhouse poles.
  Stipple all greenery with Woodland Night Green, a little Lime Green and then a little White. For Yellow area on Red birdhouse, stipple with Empire Gold. Paint words Liberty Blue with liner brush. Draw details with Black marker. Spray with finish.

Pot Full of Friendship

PHOTO ON PAGE 77

by Diane Bliss

MATERIALS:

7" clay pot

Acrylic paint
   White, Pink, Fuchsia, Moss Green, Cream
Ultra fine-tip Black permanent marker
1" checkerboard stencil
   or 1" square of sponge
Krylon® Matte finish spray

INSTRUCTIONS:

Paint top rim of pot White, let dry. Paint Green checks using stencil or sponge, let dry. Transfer 4 flower patterns evenly spaced around sides of pot 2" below rim. Paint each flower Pink. Paint wavy outlines and stamens with Fuchsia. Add Cream dots. Paint leaves Green. Below the rim use the marker to print all the good things about your friend or what you have in common or things you like to do together. Add dots to letters (pattern on page 78) after printing. Using the marker, outline flowers and leaves and draw stitch lines around the pot just below the rim and just above the bottom. Spray with a light coat of finish, let dry, repeat. Sign bottom of pot to your friend. Note: If you plant a live plant in this pot, use a liner.

Pot Full of Friendship for a Special Friend.

Husband & Wife Photo Frame

PHOTO ON PAGE 74

by Karen Greenstreet

MATERIALS:

Frame , Mat board, Photo
¾" wood button plugs
Curly or straight doll hair, ⅛" ribbon
Black Pigma® marker, Metal hanger
Clear acetate sheet (overhead projector)
Toothpick, cotton swab
Paintbrushes (#4 flat tole, liner)
Acrylic paint:
   Flesh, White, Black, Pink and Blue or
   Brown, Leaf Green, Forest Green,
   Purple, Lavender

INSTRUCTIONS:

Frame & Mat - Paint a garden of flowers around mat leaving a blank space for saying. Double load brush with Purple and Lavender and make flower petals using a leaf stroke. Dot flower centers with White or Purple. Double load brush with Leaf Green and Forest Green to paint leaves. Add Leaf Green and Forest Green vines with liner brush. Write saying with Pigma pen. Using a toothpick, dot ends of letters with Black paint.

Heads - Basecoat buttons plugs Flesh. Dot Blue, Brown or Green eyes with handle of brush. Add White highlight dots with toothpick. For a woman, add eyelashes nose and mouth with pen, make 3 Red dip dots for lips. For a man, dip cotton swab in Pink paint, blot on paper towel, press on cheeks, add eyebrows, nose and mouth with pen.

Wigs - Cut a 3" x 5" piece of cardboard. Gently wrap hair around short length about 15 times. Tie securely in center, cut opposite end. Trim and shape as needed for correct length and to make bangs. Glue wigs to heads.

Finishing - Glue heads to frame. Glue ribbon bows for woman's hair and man's bow tie. Glue mat to frame. Place acetate sheet between back of frame and photo. Tape photo in place and insert backing in frame. Attach hanger.

Nothing is more fun to receive than a personalized gift! Make button faces to match the recipient's hairstyle and eye color.

Heads. Basecoat front of the wood button with Light or Dark Flesh paint. Eyes: Dip end of small paintbrush into small amount of eye color. Dot eyes in center of face. Add tiny White highlights with toothpick or stylus.

For Man's Cheeks. Dip end of cotton swab into Pink paint. Blot off a little and press onto cheek area. Using toothpick, add White highlights for cheeks and eyes.

Using Pigma markers, add eyebrows, nose and mouth. Add wig and bow tie.

For woman, add eyelashes, nose and mouth with Pigma markers. Then add 3 dip dots of red to make lips. Add wig and bows.

Wigs. Cut 3" x 5" piece of cardboard for template. Gently wrap hair around short length of cardboard about 15 times. Tie securely in center to make gathered top of wig. Cut opposite end. Trim and shape wig as needed for correct length and to make bangs.

Leaf Stroke - Start with tole brush flat on paper and pull down ⅓ of the way. Slowly turn brush ending with brush at 90° angle.

'Friends are Flowers' Frame

PHOTO ON PAGE 77
by Julie McGuffee

MATERIALS:

10" x 10" wood frame with a 3" opening
Water based matte sealer
10" square of Brown paper
Double face tape
ZIG® Woodcraft markers
    Big & Broad Arctic - White, Yellow
    Chisel Tip - Burnt Sienna, Bright
    Green, Peacock, Violet, True Blue,
    Pumpkin, Carnation Pink, Forest Green
    Extra Fine - Black

INSTRUCTIONS:

1. Lightly sand frame and seal. Paint back of frame Arctic White and edge and border Bright Green. Trace and transfer pattern.

PAINT:

Stripes - Yellow using full width of marker.
Inside edge of opening - Burnt Sienna.
Flowers - Peacock, Violet and True Blue.
Flower Centers - Yellow, outline Pumpkin.
Daisies - Carnation Pink.
Centers - Pumpkin.
Leaves - Forest Green.
Details, lettering - Black.
Strokes on border - Black.

ASSEMBLE:

Attach photo with tape. Glue Brown paper on back of frame to seal.

Button Garden Frame

PHOTO ON PAGES 72-73
by Dorris Sorensen

MATERIALS:

Wood picture frame
Old buttons, #19 gauge wire
Dark Blue acrylic paint
Clear satin spray finish
Sandpaper
Drill and $3/32$" bit or small hammer and nail
Needle nose pliers
White craft glue

INSTRUCTIONS:

Paint frame Dark Blue, let dry. Sand edges to distress frame and make it look old. Drill holes or make holes with hammer and nail around outside edge of frame leaving spaces between the holes equal to the diameter of the buttons. Cut wire into various lengths from $1\frac{1}{4}$" to $2\frac{1}{4}$". Thread a button on each piece of wire and clamp in place with pliers. Dip the tips of wire in glue and insert in holes. Let dry overnight. Insert photo in frame.

Photo Tree

PHOTO ON PAGE 74
by Tanya Lovejoy

MATERIALS:

6" clay flowerpot, 6" foam ball
Green moss, 10 brass $\frac{1}{2}$" cup hooks
10 small round Gold frames with hangers
Pink silk flowers, Red eucalyptus
    branch, Large White berry pick
Jadelite Design Master spray paint
Fine Green glitter, Duco cement, Hot glue

INSTRUCTIONS:

Pick off any loose bark on branch. Decide on placement of photos, glue screws to the branch. Firmly wedge foam ball into pot. Insert branch into ball so it is straight and centered, glue to secure. Paint pot and branch Green. Glue moss to cover ball. Referring to photo, glue berries, single eucalyptus leaves and flowers to branch. Glue remaining berries, flowers and eucalyptus stems. Spread cement on branch and rim and base of pot, sprinkle with glitter. Place photos in frames and hang frames on hooks.

Postage Stamps Frame

PHOTO ON PAGE 75
by Mary Harrison

MATERIALS:

Wide wood frame with 5" x 7" opening
Cancelled stamps
Tissue paper, Small paintbrush
White glue, Matte acrylic spray finish

INSTRUCTIONS:

Place tissue paper over frame and trace outline of frame. Cut outside edges of paper $\frac{1}{2}$" wider and inside edges 1" wider than traced outline. Place glue in a shallow container and thin to a brushable consistency with water. Arrange stamps as desired. Brush the back of each stamp with glue, place on paper and smooth with fingers. On the inside corners, cut from the edge to the traced line. Brush frame with glue and press paper on frame. Fold excess to the back and smooth out wrinkles. Let glue dry then spray frame with 2 light coats of finish.

Candy Roses

PHOTO ON PAGE 75
by Marilyn Hargens

MATERIALS:

10 Hershey kisses
Floral wire
Green floral tape
6 silk rose leaves
Yellow plastic wrap
$1\frac{1}{2}$ yards of $\frac{3}{8}$" Yellow satin
    picot ribbon

INSTRUCTIONS:

Cut wire into 5 pieces (12", 11", 10", 9", 8"). For each rose, place flat sides of 2 kisses together and tightly wrap in a 6" square of plastic. Twist edges of plastic together under bottom kiss forming a stem. Place leaf stem and a piece of wire along side of plastic wrap stem, wrap with floral tape stretching tape tight. Make 5 roses.

Match ends of wires then wrap together with tape beginning 2" under shortest rose. Tie a multi-loop ribbon bow around bouquet.

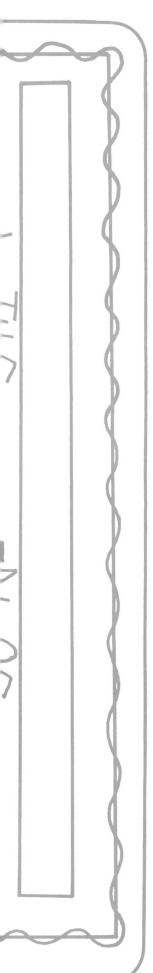

Bear Photo Frame

PHOTO ON PAGE 76

by Etsuko Suzuki

MATERIALS:

Creative Paperclay®

5" x 6" of lace fabric, Spray lacquer

2½" pieces of ⅛" Yellow and Green ribbon

Acrylic paints, Detail paintbrush, Rolling pin

White glue, Craft knife, Trash can liner bag

INSTRUCTIONS:

Frame - Cut 2 sheets of plastic from trash can liner. Roll Paperclay between sheets until it is ¼" thick. Place lace on top of Paperclay, roll over lace applying enough pressure to transfer the lace texture to the Paperclay. Peel off lace. Cut 4" x 5" rectangle of Paperclay, trim corners round. Cut out center where the picture will be and round the inside corners. There should be a ¾" margin for the frame remaining.

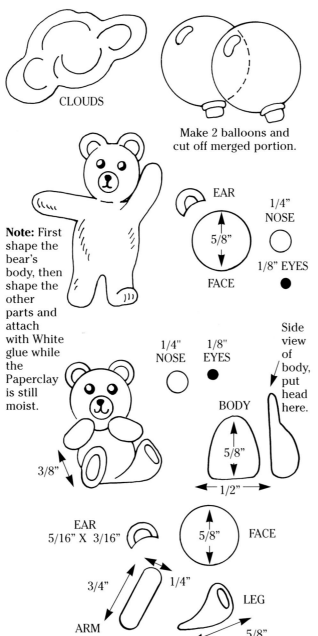

CLOUDS

Make 2 balloons and cut off merged portion.

EAR

5/8"

FACE

1/4" NOSE

1/8" EYES

●

Note: First shape the bear's body, then shape the other parts and attach with White glue while the Paperclay is still moist.

1/4" NOSE

1/8" EYES

●

Side view of body, put head here.

BODY

5/8"

1/2"

3/8"

EAR
5/16" X 3/16"

5/8"

FACE

3/4"

1/4"

ARM

LEG

5/8"

Trim - Hand shape Paperclay bears, balloons and cloud with flat backs. Let shapes and frame dry for 2 days, then paint. After paint dries, glue objects and ribbon to frame, let dry. Spray with lacquer, let dry. Glue photo to back of frame.

Toothpaste Bear

PHOTO ON PAGE 76

MATERIALS:

8" jointed plush bear

4" x 18" of patchwork print fabric

12" of ¾" Burgundy grosgrain ribbon

Travel size toothpaste tube

White oven-bake clay

White Pearl acrylic paint

2" square of White poster board

Black fine-tip permanent marker

Needle and thread

Hot glue

INSTRUCTIONS:

Cut two 4" x 9" pieces of fabric. On each piece pull threads out to fringe one 9" edge for hem of dress. With right sides together, glue short sides together leaving the top 1½" open for arm hole. Fold neck edge under ¼". Sew a gathering stitch along neck edge. Place dress on bear. Gather neck and tie to secure.

Roll a small piece of clay between your hands. Form a ¼" thick 3" long roll. Make sure one end of roll will fit into top of tube. Form a loop of clay. Bake clay following manufacturer's instructions. When clay is cool, glue end into top of tube. Paint clay White Pearl.

Using pattern, cut tooth from poster board. Use the marker to draw stitch lines around edge of tooth and write 'Good Friends Are Like Toothpaste, They Come Through In A Tight Squeeze'. Tie ribbon into a bow. Glue bow, tube and tooth to bear.

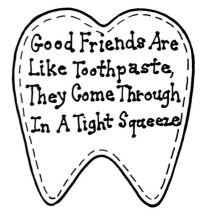

Good Friends Are Like Toothpaste, They Come Through In A Tight Squeeze

You Can't Measure Friendship

*B*ecause of my friend Janey, who is a travel agent,
*I have had the opportunity to travel to many colorful places.
Together, she and I have shared the experience of exotic
ports-of-call, unbelieveably beautiful landscapes and the fla-
vor of other cultures. When life gets hectic, Janey can look
at the smiling country doll I made for her.*

Kelley McNeill

A friend's heart is full of love.

She's an Angel and so is my friend, Muriel Spencer (right). We met at my first Society of Craft Designers Seminar as roommates. I did not know a soul and she took me under her angelic wing. Seven hundred miles hasn't kept us from sharing, caring and networking our crafts. Everyone needs an angel they can count on.

Blanche Lind

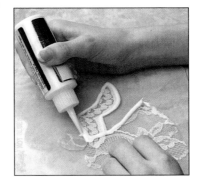

Merry Christmas!

LOVE

I still find each day too short for all the friends I want to see.

At some point in our lives if we are lucky enough, we come across a friend that has a little bit of angel in them. My friend Kathy Kappen (below) is one of those people. She collects dolls, loves flowers and the color blue. I designed this little clay earth angel with Kathy in mind. Her halo's a little bit crooked on purpose. (After all, she is just an Earth Angel!)

Kat Gonzales

My best friend Rita Anderson (left) introduced me to my husband. Rita and I even got married at the same time. She lives 2,000 miles away but we still keep in touch, especially on our mutual wedding anniversary.

Vicky Schoch

Love ourselves, love each other.

Because my mother is an avid reader and a bookmark collector, I started making them for her and including them in cards I mail to her. During her quiet reading time when she is all alone and sometimes a bit lonely, I have told her to glance at her bookmark and know that I am thinking of her and the many good times we have shared.

Donna Thomason

Jackie Brown (left) and I have been best friends for 25 years. Through many years and miles of separation we have remained close. But now we are living in the same city again and can Craft like Crazy!
Myrna Hund

Friendships are made to be treasured.

'Country Girl' Doll

PHOTO ON PAGES 82-83

MATERIALS:

14" Wimpole Street Bendi doll
5" jointed rabbit
4" of Brown doll hair, 3½" straw hat
6" Ivory Battenburg doily
⅓ yard of Green print fabric
10" x 22" of Ivory print fabric
1 yard of ¼" Green picot ribbon
Black acrylic paint, Paintbrush
Red and Black fabric markers
2½" chipwood basket
Three 3" carrots, 6 Ivory 3mm pearls
Spanish moss, Pink cosmetic blush
Lo-temp hot glue

INSTRUCTIONS:

Doll - Draw mouth with Red marker, brush blush on cheeks. Paint shoes Black, glue 3 pearls on each shoe for buttons.

Petticoat - Pull threads from one 22" edge of Ivory fabric to fray. Draw hearts with Red marker and write 'Friendship Warms the Heart' above frayed edge. Match 10" edges and glue a ¼" seam. Sew running stitch along top of petticoat. Pull on doll under arms, pull gathers tight and tie off. Glue in several places to secure.

Sleeves - Cut two 3" x 5" pieces of Green fabric. Match 5" edges and glue a ¼" seam. Fray bottom edge of sleeves. Slip sleeves on arms and glue over shoulders.

Dress - Cut 12" x 24" piece of Green fabric. Fray one 24" edge. Match 12" edges and glue a ¼" seam. Cut a 1½" slit from top of fabric on each side 6" from seam. Turn raw edges in. Fold top edge down ¼" and sew running stitch. Put dress on doll with seam in back. Pull thread tight around neck, tie off.

Collar - Cut out center of doily and pull doily over head. Cut 18" of ribbon, thread ends through back of doily, around waist and through front of doily. Tie ends in a bow with long tails.

Hair - Pull and fluff hair. Glue to top and sides of head. Tie 9" of ribbon around hair on each side. Glue hat on head.

Finish - Glue rabbit's hand to doll's hand. Glue moss and carrots in basket. Glue basket handle to doll's arm.

CUT 1½" SLIT

6" 6"

CENTER BACK

Friendship Ruler

PHOTO ON PAGE 82

MATERIALS:

18" wood ruler, 10 assorted buttons
Small scraps of Blue, Red and Green fabric
1½ yards of jute twine, HeatnBond™
Taupe acrylic paint
Black permanent marker, GOOP glue
Household iron, Soft cloth

INSTRUCTIONS:

Thin paint with water and test color on back of ruler. Wipe paint on ruler with cloth and let dry. Write 'You Can't Measure Friendship' with marker.

Following manufacturer's instructions, iron HeatnBond on fabric scraps. Trace heart patterns and transfer to paper side of HeatnBond. Cut out hearts, arrange and iron on ruler.

Glue buttons on ruler. Glue ends of 18" of jute to back of ruler. Make a 6 loop jute bow and tie to hanger with 12" of jute. Glue knot.

'She's an Angel'

PHOTO ON PAGE 84

by Blanche Lind

MATERIALS:

White and Pink tissue paper
4" square of White lace
Clear shrink art sheet
3-D foiling glue
Reverse collage glue, Gold foil
Scissors, #10 paintbrush
Hair dryer, Crystal glitter
8" of Gold cord
Gold sequin star
Air erasable pen
Paper punch

INSTRUCTIONS:

Angel - Place the shrink art sheet over pattern. Trace over pattern with foiling glue and dry with hair dryer. Press the foil Gold side up over glue, press foil down and rub firmly. Peel off.

Wing - Turn the angel over. Place White tissue paper over wings, trace along outer edge and cut out. Brush shrink art wing with collage glue, sprinkle with glitter. Place tissue paper wing on glue scrunching and creasing to fit.

Face - Trace face on Pink tissue paper. Brush shrink art face with collage glue. Place tissue paper face on glue scrunching and creasing to fit.

Body - Place lace over body of angel and trace with pen, cut out. Brush shrink art body with collage glue, place lace on glue.

Finish - Brush entire angel with collage glue, dry with hair dryer. Outline wrong side of angel with foiling glue, dry with hair dryer. Place the foil Gold side up over the angel, press foil down and rub firmly. Peel off. Cut out angel. Glue star to arm. Punch hole in wing. Tie cord through hole for hanger.

Special Friend Angel

PHOTO ON PAGE 84
by Gail Bird

MATERIALS:

22mm Natural wood bead
12" of Gold chenille stem
18" of 3" White wire edged ribbon with
    Gold edge and dashes
18" of 3" White wire edged ribbon
18" of fine wire
Gold synthetic kitchen scrubbie
½" Gold bell
Clear plastic corsage box
Pastel shredded paper
Lo-temp glue gun
Wire cutters
Needle nose pliers

INSTRUCTIONS:

Dress & Arms - Roll ends of Gold dash ribbon under ¼" to form a fine rolled hem, fold ribbon in half. Fold stem in half and twist stem around ribbon 3" from fold. Thread ends of stem through the bead. Flip the 3" loop of ribbon over head to form arms, fluff. Make a 1" circle with excess stem to form a halo on top of head. Fold 9" of wire in half and twist at center of arms. Attach bell to wire, trim excess.

Bow & Hanger - Make a White ribbon bow with 3½" loops, secure with 9" of wire and cut ribbon ends in a V. Attach bow at neck with wire and slip ends through hole in bead. Twist together to form a hanging loop.

Finish - Glue a small amount of scrubbie on head for hair. Fill box with shredded paper, place angel in box.

Angel with Wire Wings

PHOTO ON PAGE 85
by Vicky Schoch

MATERIALS:

6½" wire wings and halo
1½ wood ball knob head
Spanish moss
12" of Light Blue eyelet lace
Hot glue
Acrylic Paint
    Flesh, Peach, White,
    Black, Light Blue

INSTRUCTIONS:

Paint - Basecoat ball knob Flesh. Trace and transfer face pattern. Outline mouth, eyes and lashes with Black. Paint eyes White. Paint irises Light Blue, highlight with White. Make a Black 'tornado' then shade top half of each eye Black, add a White dot highlight above 'tornado'. Paint cheeks and nose Peach. Tightly gather top of eyelet, glue to bottom of head. Glue moss to head for hair. Glue wings and halo to back of head.

FOLD IN HALF

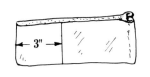

FOLD ENDS ¼" FOR FINE ROLLED HEM.

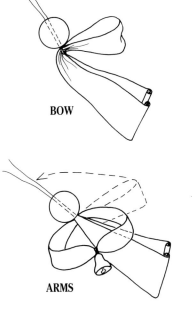

BOW

ARMS

FACE PATTERN FOR ANGEL WITH WIRE WINGS   **TORNADO**

Earth Angel

PHOTO ON PAGE 85
by Kat Gonzales

MATERIALS:

White Sculpey, Fleshtone Super Sculpey
Sculpey III
    Bronze, Light Blue Pearl, Red
Gold decorative wedding band
Beige tipped Pink carnation flower petals
#2 flat paintbrush
Paper towels, Baby oil
Toothpicks, Garlic press
Craft knife with a dull side, Straight pin
Tip: Put a little baby oil on hands then wipe off with a paper towel. Do this before you start and between colors.

INSTRUCTIONS:

Body - Shape a 3" high cone of White Sculpey. Insert handle of paintbrush in bottom pushing it halfway through cone. Roll cone back and forth in palm of your hand until it is hollowed out. Using your thumb and fingers, smooth and shape cone with bottom flaring out slightly. Cut a toothpick in half and insert cut end into top of cone leaving half of toothpick extending from top. Bake on an upside down cake pan for 20 minutes at 225°F. Remove from oven, let cool.

Hands - Roll a small ball of Fleshtone Super Sculpey into a ⅜" x 4" cylinder, cut in half. Press down slightly on one end of each cylinder to make a flat circular area. Cut out section between thumb and fingers. Make sure thumbs point inward. Make 4 more cuts to create fingers. Separate fingers by running a toothpick between each cut. Roll each finger gently between your thumb and fingers to shape.

Mark Fingers - With the head of a straight pin, press tips of each finger gently to make fingernails. With dull side of craft knife, make knuckle marks on each finger. Place dull side of knife across base of thumb inside hand and gently bend thumb up. Place knife across base of fingers and gently bend fingers over slightly. Roll base of hand

continued on page 90

Earth Angel

continued from page 89

between your fingers to form wrist.

Robe - Roll a thin layer of Light Blue clay and cut a 3¼" x 4½" piece. Overlap the 3¼" sides and smooth seam with your finger. Pull clay down over top of body. Stretch gently over bottom of body. Gather top of clay around toothpick. Do not cover toothpick.

Sleeves - Make 2 Light Blue ½" clay balls. Shape into cones and hollow out the inside. Place handle of paintbrush half way into each cone and bend top up into an L. With dull side of knife, make 2 marks at the bend for elbow. Place sleeves on each side of robe. Do not flatten. Do not push them on too hard, they will be positioned after the hands are attached.

Face - Roll a 1" Fleshtone ball for head. Shape a small Fleshtone teardrop and place in center of face for nose. Blend the top and smooth into face. Make 2 nostrils on bottom of nose with a toothpick. For mouth, insert toothpick under nose and make a small circle then bring up on each side slightly to make a nice smile. Smooth with a bit of baby oil on the tip of a paintbrush. Mix tiny bits of Red and White clay to make Pink. Make a flat Pink teardrop and place inside mouth for tongue. Place head

over top of body on toothpick.

Hair - Place Bronze clay in garlic press, press out. Place strands for bangs to the back of the head. With a toothpick gently push ends of strands into head then fold to front. Trim with knife just above nose. Starting in middle of head, place clay down one side then the other forming a part down the center. Fill in back. Make small openings in hair by pulling some strands up slightly on each side where wings will be glued in later.

Doll - Make a ⅜" Fleshtone ball. Make a tiny Fleshtone teardrop and smooth into ball for nose. Make small holes for nostrils and mouth with toothpick. Roll a thin layer of White and cut a 2" square for blanket. Place head on one end and fold bottom corner up slightly then fold left and right corners to center. Fold top corner over forehead.

Bake Angel - Place hands in sleeves, cut arms to fit. Make sure thumbs face inward. Place doll in left hand and position right arm pushing up halo. Gently brush rough edges with baby oil. Bake on an upside down cake pan for 30 minutes at 225°F. Remove from oven and let cool.

Finish Angel - For each wing, fold 2 flower petals in half, glue in opening in hair. Glue wedding band on head for halo referring to photo for placement.

Bookmarks

PHOTO ON PAGE 86
by Donna Thomason

MATERIALS:
Fabric glue

Roses:
14" of 1½" rose print satin ribbon
4" of Pink 4mm pearls-by-the-yard
4" of White scallop edge pleated lace
½" ribbon roses (2 Pink, 2 Light Green)
4 Purple ⅜" ribbon roses with leaves
4 Dusty Rose ¼" ribbon roses

White Ribbon:
14" of 1½" White satin and tulle ribbon
6" of Gold 3mm pearls-by-the-yard
9" of 2mm Iridescent pearls-by-the-yard
3" of White / Gold 6mm cord
3" of Gold loop braid
10mm x 14mm rhinestone cabochon

Tapestry:
14" of 1⅞" Black with rose print ribbon
8" of 2" Gold fringe
8" of ¼" Burgundy rose braid

Blanket Design:
14" of 1½" blanket print grosgrain ribbon
6" of 2" Cream suede fringe

Zig Zag:
14" of 1½" zig zag print ribbon
3" of 2" multi color prebeaded fringe
¾" x 7" pieces of Turquoise suede
Pinking shears

INSTRUCTIONS:
Roses - Cut lace and pearls in half, glue horizontally to cut ends of ribbon. Referring to photo, arrange and glue roses above lace and pearls.

White Ribbon - Cut Iridescent pearls, cord and braid in half. Cut Gold pearls into 4 equal lengths. On each cut end of ribbon, glue braid horizontally to ribbon with loops overlapping ends and cord and Gold pearls above braid. Glue a rhinestone centered on braid and cord. Referring to photo, loop and glue Iridescent pearls on braid.

Tapestry - Cut braid and fringe in half. On each cut end, wrap and glue fringe horizontally around ribbon. Glue braid around top of fringe.

Blanket Design - Cut four 1½" pieces of fringe. On each end, glue a fringe piece horizontally on front and back of ribbon.

Zig Zag - Cut fringe in half. Cut four ½" x 1½" pieces of suede with pinking shears. On each cut end, glue fringe horizontally on ribbon. Glue a suede piece to the front and back of ribbon covering top of fringe.

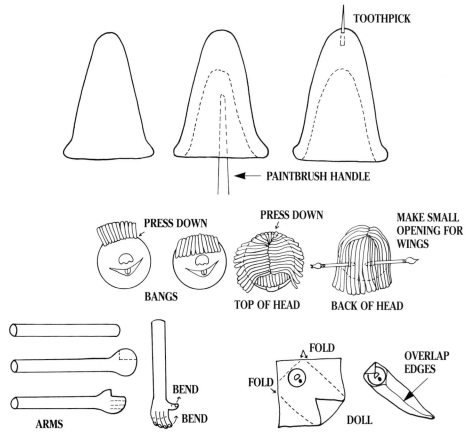

TOOTHPICK

PAINTBRUSH HANDLE

PRESS DOWN

BANGS

PRESS DOWN

TOP OF HEAD

MAKE SMALL OPENING FOR WINGS

BACK OF HEAD

ARMS

BEND

BEND

FOLD

FOLD

DOLL

OVERLAP EDGES

Red Ornament

PHOTO ON PAGE 86
by Donna Thomason

MATERIALS:

2½" Red glass Christmas ornament

12" of ¼" Green braid

2 yards of 3mm Gold pearls-by-the-yard

13 Green 8mm rhinestones

4 Green 10mm rhinestones

4 Green 8mm x 10mm rectangular rhinestones

Gold glitter hot glue

INSTRUCTIONS:

Braid - Thread loops of pearls through every other large loop of braid as shown in photo. Glue 9" of the braid with pearls on ornament just above center. Glue a length of braid with 4 pearl loops to the bottom of the ornament.

Rhinestones - Glue an 8mm rhinestone between every 2 pearl loops. Cut eight 1½" lengths of pearls and glue between rhinestones. Referring to photo, glue the 10mm and rectangular rhinestones equally spaced above braid. Cover the metal collar at the top of ornament with glue, press four 8mm rhinestones in the glue.

Hanging Loop - Cut a 6" length of pearls and thread through metal loop. Glue the ends together and glue an 8mm rhinestone in glue on each side of pearls.

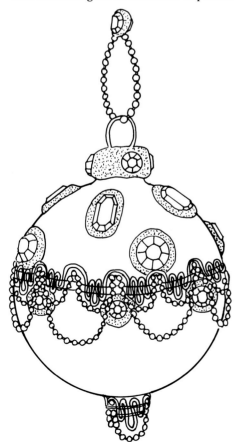

Velvet Ornaments

PHOTO ON PAGE 87
by Myrna Hund

MATERIALS:

3" styrofoam balls

Hot glue

Red Ornament:

4½" x 12" of Red velvet

4" Gold tassel

2" of Gold chain

1 yard each of Green & Gold strung sequins

2 yards of Red strung sequins

Sequin pins

Turquoise/Gold Ornament:

4½" x 12" of Turquoise velvet

12" of ½" Turquoise velvet ribbon

1 yard of ¼" Gold rickrack

1 yard of ½" Gold/Silver metallic ribbon

10mm Gold bead

Turquoise/Pearl Ornament:

4½" x 12" of Turquoise velvet

2 yards of 4mm pearls-by-the-yard

2" of 8mm pearls-by-the-yard

12" of ¼" White satin ribbon

Three 1¼" pearl medallions with fringe

INSTRUCTIONS:

For all ornaments - Trace pattern. Cut 6 velvet pieces on the bias so the fabric will stretch. Glue pieces side by side on ball stretching slightly until the ball is covered. Match the nap on all pieces. There will be 3 seams running around the ball. Cut 9¾" of trim, glue over each seam. Glue a 2" piece of ribbon or chain to top of ornament for hanger.

Red Ornament - Pin strung Gold sequins over seams. Pin rows of Green sequins between the Gold rows. Pin Red sequins between the Gold and Green sequins. Cut the hanging loop off tassel. Glue the tassel to the bottom and the chain to the top of ornament.

Turquoise/Gold Ornament - Glue Gold/Silver ribbon over seams. Glue a row of rickrack between ribbon rows. Glue 10mm bead to the bottom of ball. Make hanging loop with rick rack. Tie a bow with velvet ribbon and glue inside loop.

Turquoise/Pearl Ornament - Glue 4mm pearls around ball and over seams leaving a 1½" gap in center of each seam on one side of ball. Glue a row of pearls ¼" from each side of pearl covered seams. Glue medallions over gaps on seams. Glue 8mm pearls to the bottom of ornament. Glue a 2" ribbon loop to top of ornament. Tie bow with the remaining ribbon, glue inside loop.

Snowman

PHOTO ON PAGE 87
MATERIALS:

1½" and 4" styrofoam balls

Snow-Tex™

6" broom

3" straw hat

Red, Yellow and Black ½" buttons

2 Black snaps

1¼" Red bird

Spray glitter

1" x 13" piece of torn cotton fabric,

Lo-temp hot and White glue

Black, Flesh and Orange acrylic paint

Paintbrush

Serrated kitchen knife

INSTRUCTIONS:

Use a serrated kitchen knife to cut a small piece off the large ball to form a flat base (see diagram). Cut a smaller piece off the top of large ball and the bottom of small ball. Glue the flat side of small ball to the top of large ball with White glue. Glue scrap styrofoam to sides for arms.

Cover styrofoam with Snow-Tex. Form a carrot shaped nose. Make face smooth and texture body. Paint nose Orange, make Black dots for mouth and Flesh dots for cheeks. Spray snowman with glitter.

Pull threads from each end of fabric piece to make fringe for scarf. Wrap and glue scarf around neck. Glue snap eyes, buttons, hat, broom and bird on snowman.

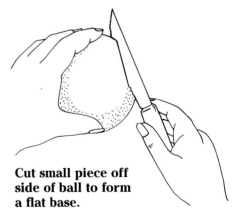

Cut small piece off side of ball to form a flat base.

My snowman gift, which holds a garland of three stars was given to honor the birth of my friend Barb's (left) third child. Our children love to play in the snow and make snow people, so I knew it would be a gift the children would enjoy too.

Mary Ayres

I treasure our friendship.

Though we are separated by many miles, my best friend Amy (right) and I have kept our friendship growing deeper though the years thanks to the U.S. Postal System. We are always sending each other pictures and small presents like this heart pocket gift.

Kathy Fatheree

Nine of us have been friends since college and our friendships have always remained strong. Every spring we begin making plans for our annual get-together. This year I'm giving each of my friends an angel ornament with a heart inscribed with the date of our last reunion. (Judy - third from left)

Judy LaSalle

Take time to see and
enjoy the wonderful
love of friendship.

As cousins, Cathy and I grew up together. We enjoyed watching our grandmother quilt. Today we still share the same interests and are best friends. 'Mee-ma' would have loved this felt heart box made in her memory.

Janie Ray

My friend Tina (right) and her family moved across town into their new house. As neighbors for nine years, we visited on the front steps almost every day. She no longer lives right next door, but my little gingerbread man can serve as a reminder of the wonderful times spent together and those yet to come on her front steps.

Debi Schmitz

friends like you are special.

One of the greatest joys of parenting is helping a young child learn what wonders they can create with their own two hands. My daughter Laurel (right) and I love to craft together. When she was 3¹/₂ years old, we designed a book called 'Mommy and Me'. I hope someday, she will pass the fun of crafting along to her children.

Lynda Musante

Although my sister, Gloria Urban (left), and I live half a country apart, it doesn't stop us from being the best of friends. Several years ago, she introduced me to beading and I haven't stopped since. We had a really good laugh the Christmas we made each other the same old fashioned Santa Claus dolls!

Carole Rodgers

Heaven's gift of love

Share Your Love

This sachet is for my friend, Mary (left) who also as luck would have it, is my mother-in-law. Mary's love and knowledge of wildflowers and her son inspired mine.

Cindy Bush Cambier

Peggy Williams (left) has been one of my closest friends for many years. She is always there when I need a helping hand, someone to confide in or need advice. Best of all, we have fun together and share many laughs.

Phyllis Dobbs

Snowman Pillow

PHOTO ON PAGES 92-93
by Mary Ayres

MATERIALS:

9" x 12" felt rectangles
Cranberry - scarf
Denim - hat and mittens
Harvest Gold - two outside stars
Antique Gold - center star
Red - hat bow
2 White - body and arms

Buttons
2 Black 3/16" flat - eyes
1 White 3/8" shank - nose
4 Metallic Gold 3/8" shank - joining stars
2 Metallic Gold 7/8" flat - outside star centers
1 Cranberry 3/4" flat - center star center
1 Cranberry 1/2" flat - hat bow

1" Light Blue pompon
Light Blue, Black, Cranberry floss
White sewing thread
Polyester fiberfill
Red acrylic paint
Stencil brush
Embroidery and hand sewing needles

INSTRUCTIONS:

Trace patterns. Use 3 strands of floss for all embroidery.

Body - Cut 2 bodies from White. Mark eye and nose dots on front, sew nose and eye buttons in place. Dip dry stencil brush in Red paint, wipe on paper towel until brush is almost dry with no brush strokes showing. Wipe brush across cheeks in a circular motion to desired shade. Embroider 'Good Friends Warm The Heart' using Black floss and small straight stitches.

Arms & Mittens - Cut four 1 3/4" squares for arms from White and 4 mittens from Denim. Pin straight edges of mittens to arms overlapping arms 1/4" and with thumbs pointing up. Blanket stitch across overlap with Light Blue floss. Pin arms to body overlapping body 1/4".

Snowman - Pin snowman front to back. Blanket stitch around body, arms and mittens leaving 4" open at bottom. Do not cut floss. Stuff firmly with fiberfill, blanket stitch opening hiding knots and ends of floss.

Stars - Cut 4 stars from Harvest Gold and 2 stars from Antique Gold. Pin sets of 2 stars together matching colors. Blanket stitch with Cranberry floss leaving a small opening on one straight edge. Do not cut floss. Stuff with fiberfill, but-tonhole stitch opening hiding knots and ends of floss. Sew 7/8" Metallic Gold but-tons to centers of Harvest Gold stars and 3/4" Cranberry button to center of Antique Gold star hiding knots and ends under buttons. Sew stars together and to mittens with 3/8" Metallic Gold buttons.

Scarf - Cut two 2" x 12" rectangles from Cranberry. Overlap short ends 1/4" and blanket stitch with Cranberry floss. Wrap scarf around neck and tie knot on left side. Cut thin strips for 1 1/2" to fringe ends.

Hat - Cut 3" x 9 1/2" rectangle from Denim. Overlap short ends 1/4", blanket stitch with Cranberry floss. Turn up brim 3/4", blanket stitch around edge. Sew running stitch through opposite edge of hat, pull tight and tie off. Sew pompon on gathers.

Bow - Cut 3/4" x 1 1/2" rectangle from Red. Wrap floss around center and pull tight, tie knot. Sew 1/2" Cranberry but-ton to center of bow and bow to right side of hat. Tack hat on head tilted to the left.

Heart & Angel Ornament

PHOTO ON PAGE 94
by Judy LaSalle

MATERIALS:

4" x 8" of Flesh felt, 3 1/2" x 7" of Red felt
7" White Battenburg lace doily
3 Red 1/2" ribbon roses, Hot glue
15" of 1/4" White satin ribbon
2 1/2" of Auburn crepe wool doll hair
Black fine-tip marker, Cosmetic blush
Needle and thread, Polyester fiberfill

INSTRUCTIONS:

Wings - With needle and thread, gather center of doily. Tie off securely. Trace head and heart patterns and cut felt. Stitch around head and heart leaving openings at top. Stuff with fiberfill, stitch shut.

Hair - Glue half of hair to back of head, bring over top and sides, glue in place. Glue roses across top of head.

Finish - Draw eyes and mouth with marker. Glue head to center of wings. Write friend's name on heart, glue on chin. Fold ribbon in half, glue to back of wings and head with ends hanging free at bottom of ornament.

BORDER CUT 1
GREEN

HEART
CUT 1
RED

HEART
CUT 1
YELLOW

BACKGROUND
CUT 1
DARK BLUE

PATTERN FOR FELT HEART POCKET

Felt Heart Pocket

PHOTO ON PAGE 94
by Kathy Fatheree
MATERIALS:
HeatnBond Lite™
Tacky glue
White and Gold embroidery floss
8" of Gold cord
9" x 12" Felt (Dark Blue, Green, Yellow, Red)
2 Gold beads
Letter beads to spell name
8" of ³/₁₆" dowel
12 assorted ½" buttons
INSTRUCTIONS:

Trace patterns on paper side of HeatnBond. Iron HeatnBond on appropriate felt colors. Cut out shapes. Fuse Green, Yellow and Red felt shapes on Blue felt. Sew running stitches around edge of heart. Referring to photo, sew on buttons, Gold beads and name beads.

Cut 5³/₄" x 7½" piece of Blue felt. Fold end over to form a 5³/₄" square. Fuse 3 edges together with a ¼" strip of HeatnBond. Pin decorated front to back with fold to the inside. Blanket stitch sides and bottom together taking care not to stitch closed area where dowel will go. Continue stitching across top but only on front piece of felt. Do not stitch pocket closed. Insert dowel. Wrap cord around dowel at least 3 times, glue cord to dowel.

Felt Heart Box

PHOTO ON PAGE 95
by Janie Ray
MATERIALS:
Beadery Adornables heart box
Two 5" squares of Brown felt
4" square of a quilt, Five ³/₈" buttons
Peach embroidery floss, White craft glue
INSTRUCTIONS:
Cover box lid with glue. Stretch and mold felt to fit around lid. Repeat for bottom of box. When glue is thoroughly dry, trim edges of felt flush with edges of box. Cut quilt square to fit top of lid. Sew on buttons referring to photo. Sew quilt piece to felt with blanket stitches.

Felt Gingerbread Man

PHOTO ON PAGE 95
by Debi Schmitz

MATERIALS:

9" x 12" of Cinnamon felt

5" x 7" of Smokey Brown Plush felt

6" squares of 2 different Brown plaid fabrics

1/2" x 12" strip of Brown plaid fabric

Buttons (two 3/8" Burgundy, three 7/16" Burgundy, four 1/2" Brown and 13 assorted Brown and Burgundy)

Beige pearl cotton, Needle

Two 6" squares of HeatnBond™

12" of 18 gauge Black craft wire

6" cinnamon stick

Craft glue

INSTRUCTIONS:

Trace patterns and cut 2 gingerbread men from Cinnamon and one from plush felt. Iron HeatnBond on back of fabric squares. Cut 2 circles and 2 hearts from one plaid and 5 hearts from other plaid fabric. Referring to photo for placement, fuse shapes on gingerbread man. Blanket stitch around hearts, straight stitch circles, cross stitch nose and stem stitch mouth with pearl cotton. Sew on buttons as shown. Pin 2 Cinnamon gingerbread men together with plush man in center and make running stitches around edge.

Wrap wire around a pencil in several places to curl, threading on buttons and inserting cinnamon stick as shown. Tie fabric strip into a bow, glue to center of cinnamon stick. Insert and glue ends of wire between hand layers.

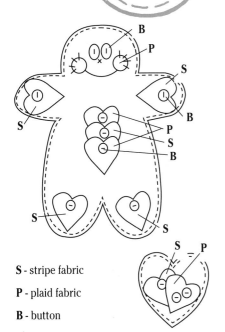

S - stripe fabric

P - plaid fabric

B - button

Moon Necklace

PHOTO ON PAGE 96
by Carole Rodgers

MATERIALS:

2" x 4" of 14 count plastic canvas

2 Gold clam shell bead tips

Gold clasp

2 Gold 6mm jumprings

Black and White embroidery floss

Beading thread and needle

Beeswax

Needle nose pliers

BEADS & CHARMS:

White seed

Black seed

White E or 6/0 seed

Black E or 6/0 seed

8 Gold 8mm

2 Black 15mm faceted

2 Black 10mm faceted

4 Gold fluted rondelles

28mm Gold sun, 13mm star

INSTRUCTIONS:

Medallion - Stitch moon on canvas following chart, cut out leaving one row of holes on all sides. Cut second piece of canvas the same size, whip stitch canvas pieces together matching floss color to bead color.

Beaded Chain (left side) - Row 1: Cut 36" of thread, run thread over wax and tie knot in one end leaving a tail. String bead tip and beads following beaded chain diagram. Pass needle through top edge hole on left side of medallion from front to back.

Row 2: Pass needle through next hole in medallion from back to front, string beads reversing pattern for Row 1. Thread through bead tip, cut thread leaving a tail.

Rows 3 & 4: Repeat beading pattern for Rows 1 and 2.

Beaded Chain (right side) - Repeat pattern for left side attaching Row 1 in top edge hole on right side of medallion. Finish: On each side, pull beads snug so seed bead sections flare out slightly, tie tails together so knot fits in bead tip, close bead tip. Attach one half of clasp to bead tip with jumpring.

Sun - Sew sun on right side of medallion, add Black seed bead in loop hole.

Fringe - Weave end of 36" of waxed thread through floss edge to secure. Pass needle through edge hole on left side of medallion. String beads for fringe strands following fringe diagram.

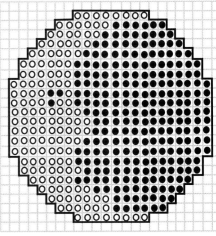

Beaded Moon Medallion

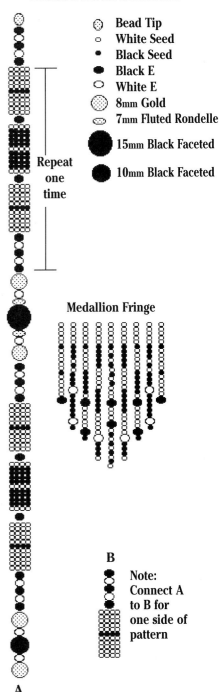

	Bead Tip
○	White Seed
•	Black Seed
■	Black E
◎	White E
	8mm Gold
	7mm Fluted Rondelle
●	15mm Black Faceted
●	10mm Black Faceted

Medallion Fringe

Note:
Connect A to B for one side of pattern

Felt Hand Pillow
PHOTO ON PAGE 97
by Phyllis Dobbs

MATERIALS:
Two 5" x 6" pieces of Blue felt
3" x 4½" of Off White felt
1½" square of Dark Red felt
4mm silk ribbon (Yellow, Light Green)
Blue embroidery floss, Large needle
Polyester fiberfill

INSTRUCTIONS:
Cut heart and hand from felt using patterns. Embroider a Yellow silk flower and Light Green leaves in center of heart. Stitch hand to the center of a piece of Blue felt and the heart to the center of the hand with Blue floss running stitches. Stack embellished piece of Blue felt on top of plain piece. Stitch around 3 sides ½" from edge with Yellow ribbon running stitches. Stuff pillow with fiberfill, stitch fourth side.

Hardware Magnet Pin
PHOTO ON PAGE 96
by Lynda Musante

MATERIALS:
1¾" doughnut magnet
8 assorted washers and locking washers
3 assorted O rings
1⅛" long spring
6" ball chain with closure
1" pin back
GOOP glue

INSTRUCTIONS:
Thread washers, O rings and spring on chain, thread chain though hole in magnet and attach closure to chain ends. Glue pin to back of magnet.

Running Stitch   **French Knot**

Felt 'Forget-Me-Not' Sachet
PHOTO ON PAGE 97
by Cindy Bush Cambier

MATERIALS:
9" x 12" sheets of felt
  Cream, Medium Blue, Moss Green
Pearl cotton (Medium Blue, Yellow/Gold)
Sewing thread (Off White, Moss Green)
Your friend's favorite potpourri - or
  scented oil and a small amount of fiberfill
Pinking shears, Scissors
Needles (sharp, chenille)

INSTRUCTIONS:
Felt - Cut three 6" x 9½" felt rectangles (2 Cream, 1 Blue), 26 Blue flowerettes, 5 Green leaves and 1 Green stem.

Flower - Use doubled Green thread, to stitch stem in place on the front Cream rectangle. Make running stitches down center of leaves, leaving the tops free. Fold the top over on 3 leaves as shown. Sew each flowerette in place with Off White straight stitches and make a Gold French knot in center.

Saying - Use chenille needle and Blue pearl cotton to running stitch 'forget-me-not' below the flower. Running stitch a heart between your friend's initials near the bottom of the back Cream rectangle.

Assemble - Stack rectangles with Blue in the center and embroidered sides to the outside. Make Blue running stitches through all layers ⅜" from edges, leaving top open and beginning 2" from top with a knot to the inside. Using pinking shears, trim all edges so Blue edging shows. Trim top edge of Blue rectangle.

Drawstrings - Cut two 26" pieces of Blue pearl cotton. With even ¼" running stitches, stitch across sachet, 2" down from top, through front 2 layers with one piece of doubled Blue pearl cotton and through back layer with the other. Use no knots and leave 12" of thread on each side. Fill sachet with potpourri or scented fiberfill. Pull thread and tie bows at each side to close top.

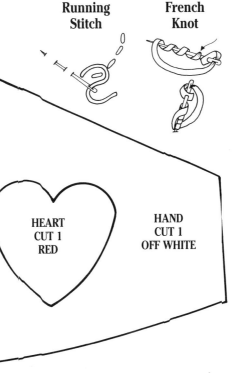

HEART
CUT 1
RED

HAND
CUT 1
OFF WHITE

forget-me-not

My sister Suzanne always says, "If it wasn't for Brendy, I would probably never have gotten moved to the country last year." After helping to organize a moving sale I painted a sign to hang near her new front door to welcome her home and remind her how special she is to me.

Brendy Kilber

Friendship can't be beat.

Little did I know when I married my husband that I was also marrying into a business partnership. My mother-in-law, Dorris Sorensen, and I have been partners for 11 years as well as great friends. I made this angel for her to show her how special our friendship is to me.

Ailese Reedy

The world is full of beauty, when the heart is full of love.

Betty (right) is the closest thing on this earth to an angel. I know I can always count on her as someone to lean on in times of crisis and as a companion to giggle with during the good times.

Jean Pedretti

From the time she was born I knew that my daughter, Tanya, (left) and I would have a wonderful friendship. She has always given me a great joy and lights up my life, just like this beehive candle. The honey is sweet (just like her), the candle's light reminds me of the sunshine she puts in my heart.

Virginia Tucker

My 5 year old grand-daughter Rachel (right) is my friend. She calls me every day after pre-school for a chat to talk about all kinds of things, but crafting is our favorite topic. She likes cutting and painting the most! "I like crafting with you Grandma", she often says. I made this little Sweet Sack for the little sweetie in my life - Rachel.

Elinor Czarnecki

Thoughtfulness is to friendship as sunshine is to a garden.

For the one I love.

This book cover was designed for a very special friend, my mother. She not only taught me to sew and embroider, but also passed along her love of reading These things and much more have brought great joy and comfort to my life. Thanks, Mom!

Linde Punzel

Friendship finds joy in forgetting what one gives, and remembering what one receives.

`My friend, Marie Ice, and I have "3 little things" in common...each of our children were born at about the same time. Marie is a talented crafter and loves handmade jewelry. My spool necklace is a token of our uncomplicated friendship. She is always there for me when I need her and vice versa.

Kathy McMillan

True friendship is worth its weight in gold.

Pat Hickenlooper (right) is my long-time, long-distance friend. I sent my handmade 'Believe in Yourself' heart to her to show how much our friendship means to me.

Dorris Sorensen

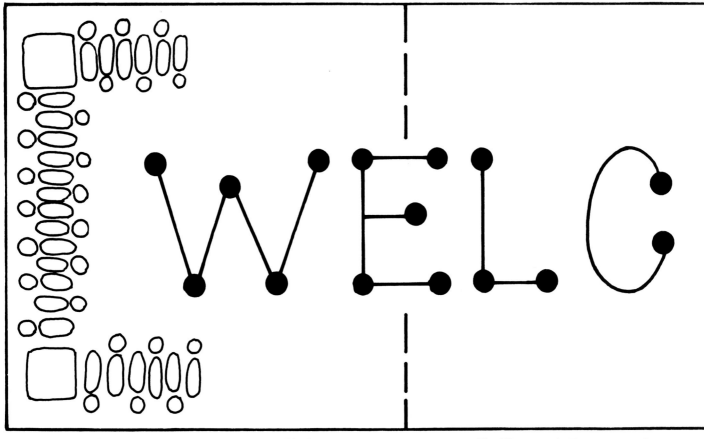

Welcome Tiles

PHOTO ON PAGE 102
by Brendy Kilber
MATERIALS:
3 White 4½" unglazed tiles
Red, Yellow, Green and Dark Blue one-
   stroke ceramic paint
7¼" x 16" pine board, Sandpaper, File
Burnt Umber acrylic paint
Spray matte acrylic sealer
3 yards of jute twine, Old toothbrush
Soft cloth, Drill with ⅛" bit, GOOP glue
INSTRUCTIONS FOR BOARD:
1. Distress ends of board with file, sand.
2. Thin paint with water. Test mixture on
   back of board. Add more water or
   paint as needed. Use a soft cloth to
   wipe mixture on edges and top of
   board. Dab paint into distress marks.
   Let dry. Apply a second coat if needed.
3. Slightly thin paint with water. Dip
   toothbrush in thinned paint, hold
   brush with bristles down over board
   and run thumb across bristles. Let
   dry. Spray with sealer.
4. Drill holes in top corners of board.
   Thread jute through one hole, even
   ends. Holding both pieces of jute
   together, tie a knot close to board. Tie
   knots at 3" intervals leaving 6" tails.
   Thread jute through second hole
   from front to back. Tie a knot on back

side of hole, trim excess jute.
5. Line tiles in a row, trace pattern.
6. Paint Welcome, corner squares and
   alternating bolder strokes Red. Paint
   other border strokes Blue. Paint inner
   dots Green and outer dots Yellow.
   When dry, take to ceramic shop to fire.
7. Glue tiles on board with GOOP glue.

Flower Pot Angel

PHOTO ON PAGE 104
by Ailese Reedy
MATERIALS:
3" clay pot,
36" of #18 wire
2" wood ball knob
2 Silver bells
Small strip of fabric
Small sponge
4 tiny Pink silk flowers
Curly crepe wool hair
Clear satin spray finish
Exterior satin varnish
White craft glue
Black fine-tip marker

6" x 7" piece of a Brown paper bag
Delta Color Accent - Tea Dye Brown
Paint brushes (¾" flat, #8 flat, #2 liner)
4 yards of ⅛" Blue satin ribbon
DELTA CERAMCOAT PAINT COLORS:
Tide Pool Blue, Liberty Blue, Ivory,
Woodland Night Green, Green Sea,
Rouge, Dunes, Black, Empire Gold
INSTRUCTIONS:
   Head - Paint pot inside and out with 2
coats of exterior varnish. Paint ball knob
with 2 coats of Dunes. Using a small
piece of sponge, sponge cheeks Rouge.
When dry, using #2 liner, paint eyes
Black. Add Ivory sparkle dots to eyes and
cheeks. Add face details with Black mark-
er. Spray with one coat of satin varnish.
   Pot - Using #8 flat brush and watered
down Green Sea, dab leaves around pot.
When dry, dab watered down Woodland
Night on leaves. Using #2 liner and Ivory,
pull 4-petal flowers, dot centers Empire
Gold, add Liberty Blue dots. Outline all
designs with Black marker. Double dip a
½" square of sponge in Liberty Blue and
Tide Pool Blue and make checkerboard
design around bottom edge of pot.
   Legs & Hanger - Bend wire in half and
wrap ends around a pencil to form coils
for legs. Attach a bell to bottom of each
coil. Cut 16" of ribbon, fold in half. Tie
ends around center of legs. Thread fold

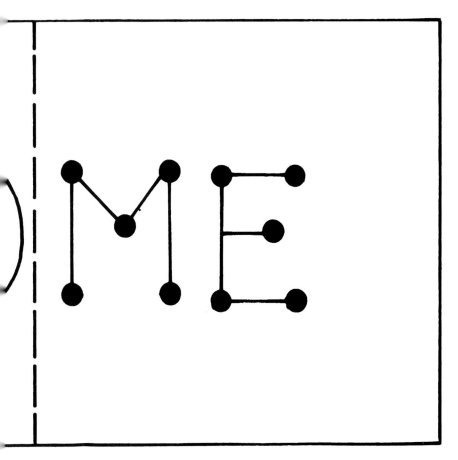

tie a raffia shoestring bow with 3" loops. Pull loops tight and adjust size. Glue below head. Split strands into narrow pieces. Glue moss hair from ear to ear and down back of head. Trim if necessary. Tie fabric bow. Glue bow on angel. Glue star on bow.

Watermelon Box
PHOTO ON PAGE 104
by Laura Kievlan
MATERIALS:
3" x 4" oval shaker box
Acrylic paint -
   Off White, Red, Dark Green, Light Green
Black dimensional paint
Small flat paintbrush, Small sponge
Black fine-tip permanent marker
INSTRUCTIONS:
   Basecoat top of lid Off White. Basecoat lid sides and outside of box Dark Green. Referring to photo, sponge Light Green stripes on sides of lid and sides of box. Sponge Red in center of lid leaving a White rim around edge. Add seeds with Black dimensional paint.
   With Black marker, write 'Friendship Seeds' in center of lid, write 'To' and 'From' on sides of box.

through hole in pot and through head. Glue ribbon in place. Glue knob to top of pot.
   Trim - Tie a small fabric bow and glue under chin. Glue hair on head. Form pony tails and tie close to base of head with small pieces of ribbon.
   Wings - Fold Brown paper in half to 3" x 7". Using a lot of glue, spread evenly over one side and press sides together. When glue is dry, wad paper to form as many creases and wrinkles as possible. Leave wadded and spray both sides with with Floral Accent Tea Dye Brown, let dry and repeat. Partially flatten wings and glue in place. Cut remaining ribbon in half. Tie a loopy bow with remaining ribbon and glue on top of wings. Glue flowers at base of wings.

Coke Bear
PHOTO ON PAGES 102-103
MATERIALS:
10" jointed bear, Coke bottle
18" of 7/8" Dark Green wire edge ribbon
2" wood heart, 2 Red straws
Red acrylic paint, Paintbrush
Black fine-tip permanent marker
3/4" Yellow ribbon rose, GOOP glue
INSTRUCTIONS:
   Tie ribbon bow around neck. Glue rose to bow. Wrap bear's paws around bottle and glue in place. Paint heart

Red. Write 'Friends Go Better With Coke' with marker. Glue heart between bear's hands.

Bobbin Angel
PHOTO ON PAGE 104
by Jean Marie Pedretti
MATERIALS:
8" quill or pirn bobbin, Paintbrush
3" wood heart (base), 1" wood star
2" wood ball knob (head)
1" x 27" strip of torn Green print fabric
15 strands of Natural raffia
Acrylic paint - Green, Gold, Black, White
Pink cosmetic blush, Cotton swab
Drill and 3/8" or 1/2" bit, GOOP glue
BODY ASSEMBLY:

1. Drill hole in center of flat side of ball knob. Glue top of bobbin in hole, tap in with hammer if necessary. Glue heart on bottom of bobbin. Let glue dry for 24 hours.
2. Paint eyes and mouth Black, dot eyes White. Rub cheeks with blush. Paint star Gold and heart Green. For wings,

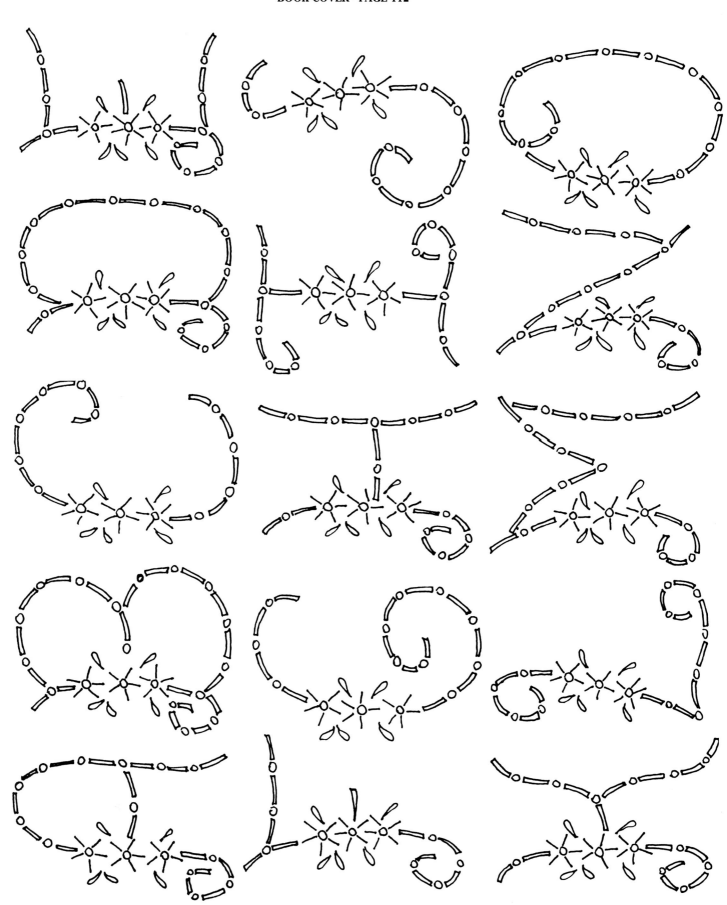

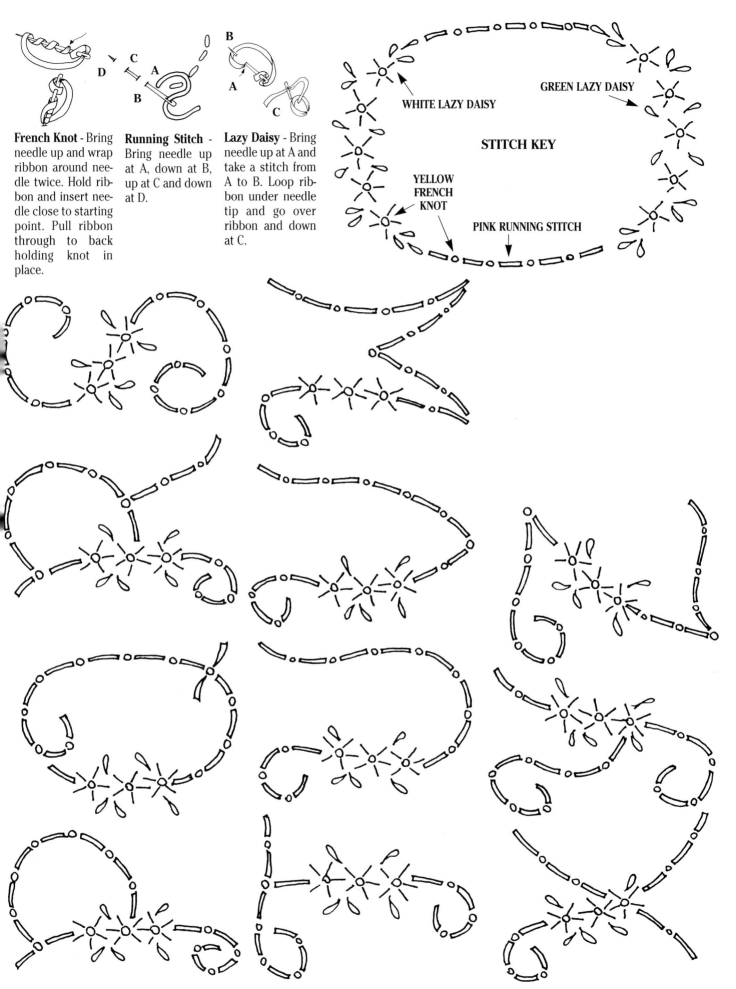

French Knot - Bring needle up and wrap ribbon around needle twice. Hold ribbon and insert needle close to starting point. Pull ribbon through to back holding knot in place.

Running Stitch - Bring needle up at A, down at B, up at C and down at D.

Lazy Daisy - Bring needle up at A and take a stitch from A to B. Loop ribbon under needle tip and go over ribbon and down at C.

STITCH KEY

WHITE LAZY DAISY

GREEN LAZY DAISY

YELLOW FRENCH KNOT

PINK RUNNING STITCH

Ribbon Embroidery Book Cover

PHOTO ON PAGE 106
ALPHABET Patterns on pages 110-111
by Linde Punzel

MATERIALS:
8" x 17" cranberry moire fabric
8" x 17" print fabric
8" x 17" iron-on interfacing
8" of 1½" grosgrain ribbon
Sewing thread, Embroidery hoop
Silk ribbon or chenille needle
4mm silk ribbon (White, Yellow,
    Green, Pink)

INSTRUCTIONS
Center monogram in border design and transfer to moire fabric 6½" from right side of fabric (pattern on pages 110-111). Place in hoop. Embroider following stitch key.

Iron interfacing to wrong side of print fabric. Pin ribbon to right side of fabric 5" from right edge.

Place cover and print fabric right sides together and stitch ¼" from all edges, catching in ribbon and leaving an opening for turning. Turn right side out with ribbon to print side. Press. Slip stitch edge.

Fold in a 4" flap on monogramed side of cover. Slip stitch top and bottom edges to form pocket. Slide front cover of book into pocket and back cover under ribbon. Fold remainder in to keep your place.

Rag Angel

PHOTO ON PAGE 106
by Amy Alexander

MATERIALS:
1½ yards of muslin
Pair of 7" Gold metallic angel wings
1 yard of ¼" Burgundy satin ribbon
2 yards of 4mm Gold pearls-by-the-yard
Small silk flowers
Spanish moss (for hair)
Black fine tip permanent marker
Pink cosmetic blush
Sewing thread and needle
Polyester fiberfill
9" of wrapped craft wire (for halo)
Lo-temp glue

INSTRUCTIONS:
Tear muslin into forty 1" strips.

Body - Cut 7 muslin strips in half. Twist 12 pieces together slightly to form arms. Fold center of 31 strips over cen-

ter of arms. Tie tightly under arms with a half strip, tie bow in back. Glue and wrap hands together with remaining half strip, let tails dangle.

Head - Cut a 6" circle from muslin. Sew a running stitch ¼" from edge of muslin circle, place fiberfill in center, pull stitches tight and tie off. Draw face with marker, rub cheeks with blush. Glue moss on head for hair.

Halo - Twist ends of wire together. Wrap wire with Gold pearls-by-the-yard. Glue ends to wire. Glue on head.

Wings - Glue wings on back.

Trim - Tie a bow with Burgundy ribbon and Gold pearls. Glue pearls, flowers and ribbon bow on hands.

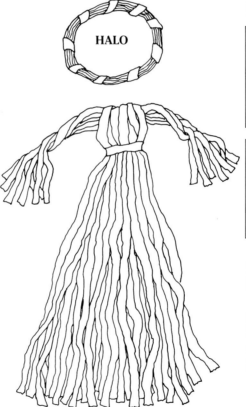

RAG BODY

BEE WINGS

BEEHIVE CANDLE PATTERNS

Beehive Candle

PHOTO ON PAGE 105
by Virginia Tucker

MATERIALS:
2 sheets of Natural beeswax
Seven ⅜" wood beads
Seven Black E beads
Yellow acrylic paint
6" of ⅜" White Iridescent floral ribbon
Toothpick
1½" Red wood heart
Black fine-tip permanent marker
Lo-temp hot glue

INSTRUCTIONS:
Candle - Stack sheets of Natural wax, cut 2-layer pieces as shown. Roll largest piece around wick making sure wax is tight and even around wick. Roll remaining pieces overlapping ends 1". Heat a pie pan on stove burner, remove from heat and press candle in pan to level bottom of candle.

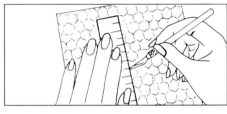

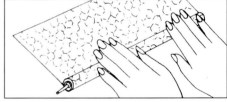

Heart - Write message on heart with Black marker. Glue toothpick to back of heart. Insert end of toothpick in candle.

Bees - Paint wood beads Yellow. Make stripes with Black marker. Glue an E bead over one hole on each bead. Cut wings from ribbon, glue to top of bead. Glue bees to candle.

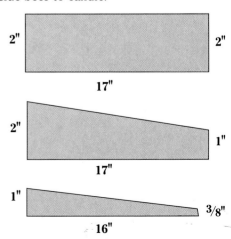

Spool Necklace

PHOTO ON PAGE 107

MATERIALS:
27" of ¼" Dark Green satin ribbon
2 Natural 10mm wood beads
4 Burgundy 16mm wood beads
1¾" and two 1¼" spools
Ivory, Black and Burgundy acrylic paint
Paintbrush

INSTRUCTIONS:
Paint ends of small spools Black and large spool Burgundy. Paint center of spools Ivory, let dry. Trace heart patterns and transfer to spools. Paint hearts on large spool Black and small spools Burgundy. Paint dots and stitch lines Black. Thread spools and beads on ribbon referring to photo. Tie ends of ribbon in a bow.

*Happy is the heart
that shelters a friend.*

'Believe in Yourself' Heart

PHOTO ON PAGE 107

by Dorris Sorensen

MATERIALS:
4" x 8" and 3" x 5" pieces of wood
One 3" and two 36" pieces of #18 wire
Assorted buttons
Clear satin spray finish, White craft glue
Black fine-tip permanent marker
Paint brushes (#4 flat, #2 liner, ¾" flat)

DELTA CERAMCOAT PAINT COLORS:
Barn Red, Antique White
Liberty Blue, Navy Blue

INSTRUCTIONS:
Hearts - Using patterns, cut one of each heart from balsa wood or foam core. Basecoat hearts with 2-3 coats of paint. Large heart is Liberty Blue, small heart is Barn Red. Trace and transfer words to large heart. Using liner brush and watered down Antique White, paint words and outline with Black marker.

Hanger - Wrap one 36" piece of wire around a pencil adding buttons to some coils to form hanger. Push ends of hanger from the back to the front of the large heart at the dots. Twist small loops to secure. Bend other 36" piece of wire into a bow, secure center of bow with 3" piece of wire. Attach bow to center loop of hanger.

Our Friendship Keeps Budding Through The Years
Friends are so TWEET

They say birds of a feather flock together. My friend Barbara and I have spent many a pleasant afternoon together enjoying each other's company. She loves Victorian Collectables and I love to paint. So voila - a new birdhouse to add to her collection.
De De Stanley

Plant kindness,
harvest love

The heart that gives gathers.

I made these 'House Shoes' for my friend, Dee Dee (left). Even though our houses are in different towns, we've remained friends since childhood.

Two little houses sitting on a shoe,
One is me and the other is you.
When you stand still, two houses side by side.
The distance between us is not very wide.

When you slip us on
And walk about all day,
We pass each other often
As we go along our way.

And when at night
Through dreams we glide,
They sit on the floor,
Side by side.

Even though as friends we're very far apart,
Two houses, two hearts, two different people,
We will forever be as one
Deep within our hearts.

Vivian Peritts

I have nine children and I am proud of each and every one of them. Recently I began making a 'village' using my children's occupations and hobbies as themes for the shops. My husband Jim cuts out the shapes and I paint them during the long Wisconsin winters. My son Robert (left) owns his own furniture making business - Robert's Workbench. This is the shop he inspired. I always give the original to the person who inspired the building and I make another to add to my growing village.

Joan Hubatch

My friend Jude and I enjoy life's simple pleasures . . . birds, sweet songs and the beauty of flowers. Friends like Jude enrich our lives and are the flowers in life's garden!

Linda Jordan

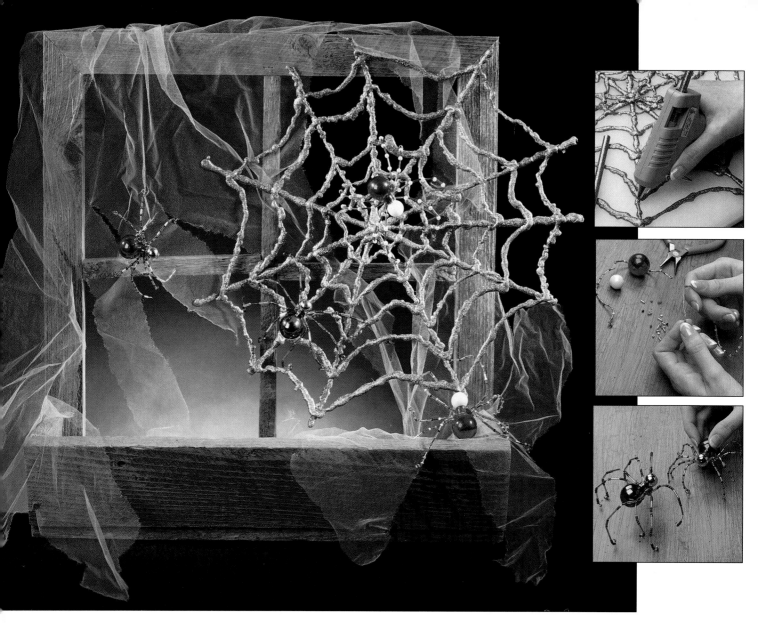

"Friendship is a heaven sent shelter from the cold."

As a professional crafter, my designs are often inspired by children. Matt (left) was 4 years old when we became fast friends. Recently he came to my rescue when I needed an idea for an unexpected television appearance. Matt taught me how to bead the spider and the idea of our spider needing a web came to me during the beading lesson.

Friendship and crafting have a lot in common. Both are all about caring, sharing and having fun with others. Both are blinded to gender, race and background. Both friendship and crafting make the world a better place to live in.

Matt shared a story about this wonderful spider. The spider found a lovely Christmas tree in a warm love-filled home and was so happy to find shelter from the cold that it spun webs all night to decorate the tree. Just before dawn an angel came down from heaven and turned the silky threads to gold. Matt and I think friendship is a heaven sent shelter from the cold.

Maria Nerius

I designed this project with my 'sisters' in mind. The Country Kitchen Hanger is dedicated to Jackie (right) and Jean (left), my best friends. They've always been there for me and this is a small scale token of my appreciation. Bay leaves symbolize honor, hearts symbolize love and the words say it all.

Jan Chase

Flower Pot & Plant Poke

PHOTO ON PAGES 114-115
by Deborah Scheblein

MATERIALS:

3½" clay pot
Three ½" wood buttons
Three 1" wood stars
3" wood heart
Popsicle stick
5" of jute
Ceramcoat Paint (Antique White, Black, Bright Yellow, Cape Cod Blue)
Ceramcoat Gloss Varnish

INSTRUCTIONS

Paint: Clay Pot - Antique White with Cape Cod Blue accents.
Wood Stars - Cape Cod Blue.
Wood Buttons - Bright Yellow.
Popsicle Stick - Cape Cod Blue.
Wood Heart - Antique White with Cape Cod Blue accent lines and Black lettering.

After painting is completed and dry, apply the Ceramcoat Gloss Varnish to each piece.

Finish - Glue two stars to the clay pot for flower petals. Glue a button to the top of each star for center of the flower. Glue one star and button to the top right hand corner of the heart. Glue the popsicle stick to the back of the heart to form the plant poke.

Separate the jute into 3 pieces. Tie each piece into a small bow. Glue a bow to the base of the heart on the plant poke. Glue the remaining bows under the flowers on the pot for leaves.

Our Friendship Keeps Budding Through The Years

'Friends Are So Tweet' Victorian Birdhouse

PHOTO ON PAGE 114
by De De Stanley

MATERIALS:

Birdhouse
DecoArt Decorating Paste and Decorating Tip Kit
DecoArt acrylic paint (Hauser Dark Green, Eggshell, Burgundy, Light Buttermilk, Hauser Medium Green, Glorious Gold)
Paintbrushes (¾" flat, #8, #4 shader)
Palette knife
Matte spray sealer

INSTRUCTIONS:

Following label instructions, place petal tip (exclamation point shape) on decorating bag. Use palette knife to put paste in bag. To form ribbon, use the flat tip. Place tip perpendicular to surface with one end touching surface. Beginning at upper left of roof and referring to photo, bring tip down roof and front of birdhouse in graceful arcs.

To form base petals, rest the large end of the tip on the surface, point narrow end to outside, raised off the surface, and squeeze the bag. As the petal begins to form, pivot the narrow end around and down in an arc, ending with it flat on the surface. Hesitate so paste fans out then move back as you stop pressure. Repeat on the left side.

To form outer petals, hold bag in same position with wide end of tip touching inside right edge of base. Start pressure, moving the narrow end out to the right in an arc. Stop pressure bringing tip back down around base. Pull tip away. Repeat for left side.

To form leaves, use the leaf tip (which has 2 sides with deep V cuts, a small side with no cut and a small side with a small cut). Lightly place the side with no cut on the surface. The small V cut side faces the ceiling and forms the vein. Hold bag at a 45° angle with the back of the bag facing you. Squeeze and hold tip in place to let paste fan out into base. Stop pressure as you pull tip straight up and away. Let all flowers and leaves dry.

PAINT:

Basecoat body of birdhouse Eggshell, roof, base and perch Hauser Dark Green. Paint ribbon Eggshell. For roses, lay Burgundy and Light Buttermilk on palette. Paint some Burgundy and then with a dirty brush pick up Light Buttermilk creating a beautiful Mauve. You can create many different values with these 2 colors. For leaves, lightly touch with Hauser Medium Green and then with a dirty brush pick up a touch of Light Buttermilk for a lighter value. Touch your finger in Glorious Gold and lightly touch over ribbon, roses and leaves to antique. Paint saying Mauve. Let paint dry and then spray house with 2 coats of finish.

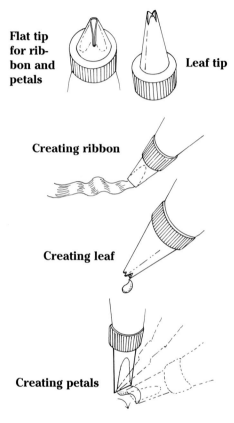

Flat tip for ribbon and petals

Leaf tip

Creating ribbon

Creating leaf

Creating petals

Friends are so TWEET

House Shoes

PHOTO ON PAGE 116
by Vivian Peritts

MATERIALS:

Green slippers

9" x 12" felt sheets (Grey, Tan, Blue, Pumpkin, Black, Brown)

Pearl dimensional paint (White, Dark Brown, Orange, Green, Pink, Purple, Yellow)

4 Gold 4mm beads

1 skein of Antique Gold embroidery floss

12" x 18" HeatnBond™

Pinking shears

Grey sewing thread

1 ounce of polyester fiberfill

INSTRUCTIONS:

1. Using pinking shears, cut two 3¾" x 2½" house tops, four 2" square house sides and four 2" x 3" house ends from Grey felt. With pinked edges on the outside, machine stitch the 4 corners of the houses together in a 1/16" seam.

2. Fuse HeatnBond on back of remaining felt pieces following manufacturer's instructions. Cut four 3¾" x 2½" roof pieces from Tan, two 5/8" x 1½" doors from Blue and two from Brown, six ½" x ¾" window from Black, six ¾" x ¾" shutters from pumpkin, two ½" round windows from Black and six ¼" x ¾" window boxes from Brown.

3. Remove paper from fused pieces. Fuse Brown doors to center back of both houses and Blue doors to side of house fronts, one on left and one on right. Fuse a shutter in center on each side of houses, a window in center of each shutter and a window box below each window. Fuse round windows to top of house fronts. Sew house tops to top of each house. Stuff house with fiberfill.

4. Fuse 2 roof pieces together, repeat for remaining 2 pieces. Fold roofs in half, iron and trim edges even. Starting at bottom on one side and working to top, stitch around edges and make shingles with blanket stitch using 3 strands of floss. Make 7 rows with ½" deep and 5/8" wide stitches. Repeat for other side.

5. Sew beads for door handles. Sew roof to top of each house and houses to slippers.

6. Outline windows, panes, round windows and doors with White paint,
shutters with Orange paint and sides and bottoms of window boxes with Brown. Use Pink, Yellow and Purple dots for flowers and Green for leaves.

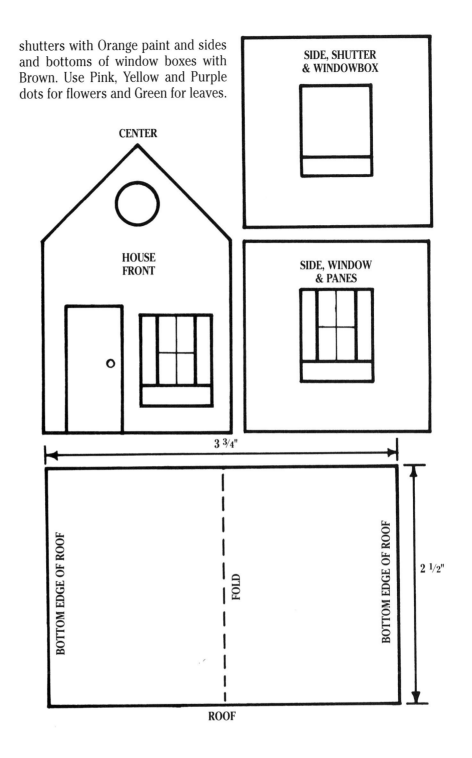

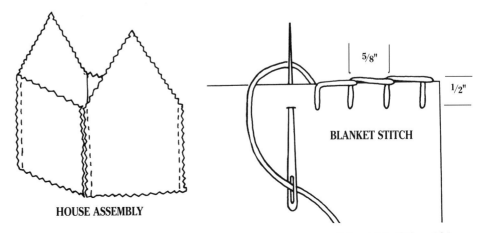

HOUSE ASSEMBLY

BLANKET STITCH

'Friends are Flowers' Door Hanger

PHOTO ON PAGE 117

by Linda Jordan

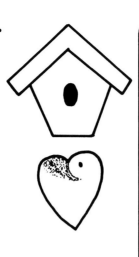

WOOD PARTS:

Door hanger
1" split pot
¾" heart (small bird)
⅜" thick chalet birdhouse
1 rectangle (shelf)
2 friends bodies (supports)
2½" of ⅛" dowel

MATERIALS:

'Friends are Flowers…' rub-on saying
Acrylic paint -
   Terra Cotta, Dark Red, Off White,
   Dark Grey, Black, White, Dark Green,
   Light Green, Burnt Umber
Paintbrushes -
   #6 Flat Shader
   Rake,
   Old toothbrush
Small bunch of dried flowers
Spanish moss
Wood glue
Small plastic eggs

INSTRUCTIONS:

Trace patterns.

PAINT:

Door hanger - Off White.
Bricks - load brush with thinned Red, 80% water
   and 20% paint. Lightly brush width of paint-
   brush on surface.
Transfer window pattern.
Window - Dark Grey, shade left side with Black.
Frame - Burnt Umber.
Trim, pane lines - White. Lightly add White
   reflection lines with rake brush.
Shelf and supports - Burnt Umber.
Pot - Terra Cotta. Spatter Red with toothbrush.
Birdhouse - thinned Burnt Umber.
   Roof - Dark Green.
   Hole - Black.
   Pole - Light Green.
Birds - Red, shade wings and tail feathers Black.
Eye - dot Black.
Beak - Black.

ASSEMBLE:

Rub saying on door hanger. Spray with sealer.
Form a small nest of Spanish moss, glue on shelf.
Glue wood parts referring to photo. Glue eggs in
nest. Glue small bunch of flowers in pot. Let dry.
Spray again with sealer.

The tranquility of sentimental moments of friendship brings thoughts of loved ones to our hearts.

Country Kitchen Hanger

PHOTO ON PAGE 119
by Jan Chase

MATERIALS:

Two 3 ounce packages of bay leaves or olive leaves
14 assorted wood hearts (¾"-2")
5 assorted Mauve and Blue fabric scraps
Mauve and 2 shades of Blue acrylic paint
Natural raffia
Dried flowers (optional)
Mod Podge
20" of ½" dowel
Stove pipe wire
White fabric paint writer
Black fine-tip permanent marker
Hot glue

INSTRUCTIONS:

Paint hearts referring to photo for colors, let dry. Trace 5 hearts, including largest heart, onto fabric scraps, cut out. Paint a thin coat of Mod Podge on traced hearts, cover with fabric heart cut outs, let dry.

Braid raffia for 19" leaving 5" frayed on each end. Secure ends with raffia ties or rubber bands. Glue dowel along center back of braid for stability. Glue bay or olive leaves on braid working from center out.

Write 'Trust', 'Love', 'Loyal', 'Gentle', 'Kind', 'Hope' and 'Honest' on painted hearts with Black marker. Using paint writer, personalize largest heart. Referring to photo, arrange hearts and glue in place. Curl two 36" pieces of wire around a pencil and attach to ends of dowel for hanger. At top center of hanger place a raffia bow and a large personalized heart. Add dried flowers or any natural accent to finish your project.

CUT TWO

KIND
HOPE
Gentle
Loyal
Love
HONEST
Trust

Wood Village

PHOTO ON PAGE 117

by Joan Hubatch

MATERIALS:

16" of 1" x 4" White pine

Saw, Wood carving knife

Sandpaper

Acrylic paint (White, Brown, Light Blue, Dark Red, Gold, Yellow, Light Grey, Grey, Silver, Black, Light Green, Dark Green, Terra Cotta, Beige, Light Brown)

INSTRUCTIONS:

Church - Cut 5" of wood. Saw basic shape. Carve out steeple and cross. Basecoat White.

Paint:

Bell rope, roof, door and window frames - Brown.

Doors - Light Brown.

Tall windows, round window and bell opening - Light Blue.

Tops of windows - Dark Red.

Dove and window panes - White.

Rays above dove - Yellow.

Steps and shading on steeple - Light Grey.

Lines between boards and steps - Grey.

Bell - Silver with Black shading.

Crosses and door handles - Gold.

Shop - Cut 4" of wood. Saw basic shape. Carve out chimneys. Basecoat Beige.

Paint:

Roof and upper door frame - Brown.

Doors - Dark Green with Black line down center.

Door handles - Yellow.

Windows - Light Blue.

Bottom door frame, window frame, lines around sign and chimneys - Terra Cotta.

Sign letters - Dark Green.

Letters on window - Black.

Chair in window- Light Green.

Table in window - Light Brown.

House - Cut 3" of wood. Saw basic shape. Carve out chimney. Basecoat Light Green.

Paint:

Roof - Brown.

Step, chimney - Grey.

Door knob and window panes - Light Blue.

Door and window frames - Terra Cotta.

Flowers - Yellow with White dot centers and tiny Terra Cotta dot highlights.

Leaves and stems - Dark Green.

Tree - Cut 3½" of wood. Cut out shape, basecoat Green.

Paint:

Leaves - Green. Shade with Dark Green.

Trunk - Brown. Shade with Black.

Lamp - Cut shape from scrap wood.

Paint:

Lamp - Black.

Glass panes - Yellow.

Concho Barrette

PHOTO ON PAGE 116

MATERIALS:

Three 2" oval conchos

4 Red ¼" ribbon roses

½" Red ribbon rose

6 silk rose leaves

1" x 2" piece of felt

3" barrette

GOOP glue

INSTRUCTIONS:

1. Glue 2 conchos with edges touching to back of remaining concho, let dry. Open barrette, remove bar. Glue barrette to conchos. Glue felt over barrette. Replace bar.

2. Trim rose leaves. Referring to photo, glue leaves and roses on conchos.

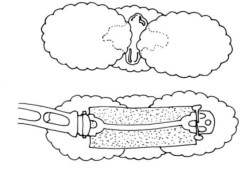

Spiders

PHOTO ON PAGE 118

by Maria Nerius & Matt McAteer

MATERIALS:

For Each Spider:

1" glass Christmas ornament

½" plastic bead

Four 7" pieces of 24 gauge wire

Bugle and seed beads or 4mm pearl beads

Lo-temp hot glue

Web:

5 to 10 sticks of lo-temp Gold glitter glue

Non stick cooking spray

Large smooth work area

INSTRUCTIONS:

Spider Body & Head - Remove ornament hanger. Glue ½" bead to ornament covering opening.

Legs - Find center of each wire. Thread beads on wires leaving ¼" space in center of wire to glue legs to body. Reverse beading pattern for other side of legs, curl both ends of wire to keep beads in place.

Assemble - Place a small amount of glue between head and body and press unbeaded wire centers in glue. Allow glue to set. Bend legs to shape.

Web - Coat work surface with non stick spray. Make the long straight lines of web first then add the curved lines. Allow glue to set. Gently peel web off work surface. If any part of web breaks repair with glue.

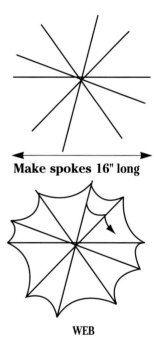

Make spokes 16" long

**WEB
MAKE STRAIGHT LINES
ADD CURVED LINES**

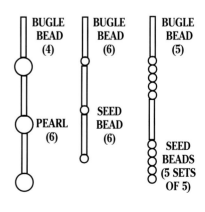

**BEADING PATTERN
FOR SPIDER LEGS**

WOOD VILLAGE PATTERNS

ROBERTS WORKBENCH

Hand Crafted Furniture

MARY'S SOAPS

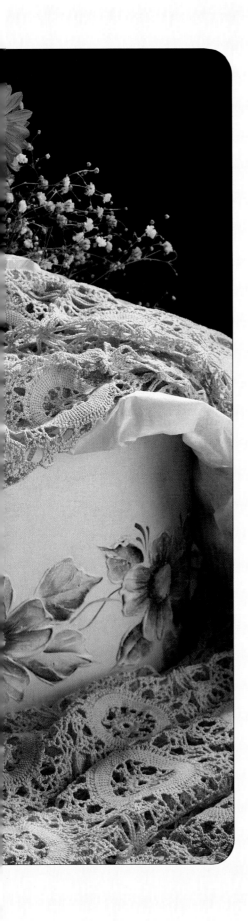

*T*he pastel floral box was painted for my sister-in-law, Joan Hoover (left) of Emporia, Kansas. It is a 'thank you' for the many years she devoted to the care of my mother. She has loved my brother more than life itself. She is not only a great and loving wife, mother, grandmother and sister, she has been one of my best friends for over 50 years. Believe it or not, we like and love each other.

Doxie Keller

The best of friends

Good friends
are
heaven's gift.

My Mom (left) is one of my very best friends. At 86, she provides transportation, home cooked meals and visits shut-ins...does volunteer church work, bowls, gardens and entertains. One problem that she's managed to pass on to me is remembering where we put things. My gift will help her keep track of her glasses and focused on all the important things in her life.

Jean Gaston

When I designed this cute little guardian angel, I was thinking of the wonderful friendship I have developed with my little grandson, Collin. He is our first grandchild and is very special to Larry and me. I will always want a guardian angel to watch over him as he grows. I will now have to make another angel for my new granddaughter, Madison. How lucky can I be, to have two precious little friends?

Judy Lindquist

These sachets were made especially for our mom, Helen (center). Since our mom designs craft items professionally, we thought a handmade item would be the ideal gift for her. Our mom is always designing or making something. These sachets are extremely easy and quick to make. They can be made with scraps of fabric and to coordinate with the decor of any room.

Laura & Melissa Rafson

Home is where the heart is.

Jenny Donalson (right) is my special friend with whom I share my joys and sorrows. Our friendship is not based on judgement, domination or control, but loyalty, generosity and acceptance.

Kathy Krystosik

This project was created for the 'best-est' person anyone would care to know, Judy McKinney (right). She and I met at a quilting class she was teaching. You might say, we have sewn up a beautiful friendship. I would like to pamper Judy with a quilting magazine, a cup of hot chocolate, a rose and 'a-death-by-chocolate' candy bar served on this tray I made especially for her.

Margaret Hanson

A friend loves at all times.

Karen (right) and I have been friends through good and bad the past 15 years. When Karen's mother passed away just before Christmas, it was very hard to know what to say. The one thing I did know was that now more than ever Karen needed to know her guardian angel was watching her and would be there for her.

Kimberly Thomas

My husband and I attended a family reunion. We enjoyed reminiscing, crisp fall weather, colorful trees and short hikes. For Thanksgiving I sent everyone a little autumn clothespin angel made from nature's treasures as a reminder of our fun-filled family gathering.

Nancy Bell Anderson

If Friends Were Flowe[r]
I'd Pick You

Pastel Floral Box

PHOTO ON PAGES 126-127
by Doxie Keller

MATERIALS:

Large oval bentwood box

4 ounces of DecoArt decorating paste

White Wash acrylic paint

DecoArt wood sealer

DecoArt Heavenly Hues - Moon Yellow, Golden Halo, Angel Flesh, Beautiful Burgundy, Patina Green, Hunter Green, Country Blue, Heavenly Grey

Loew-Cornell Paintbrushes, series 798 - ¾", 801# liner, 7300 #10 flat shader

DecoArt spray finish/sealer

Green fine tip permanent marker

Palette knife

Sponge

INSTRUCTIONS:

Load decorating paste on palette knife. Apply paste as if spreading peanut butter on bread. The paste is pulled, pushed and squeezed. Refer to diagram for direction of palette knife. Work to give leaves and petals a lot of texture. Let dry overnight. Mix equal parts of wood sealer and White paint. Paint box and designs with 2 coats of mixture working it into all the designs. Allow to dry.

PAINT:

Apply Heavenly Hues in layers. Start with the lightest color and add 2 or 3 layers for a darker value or add a darker color over a lighter color. The paint may be wiped away with a soft cloth or cotton swab. Wiping the color gives a nice effect on a textured or dimensional surfaces.

Leaves - Basecoat left side with Hunter Green and right with Patina Green. Add touches of Burgundy and Golden Halo. Let dry. Add touches of Moon Yellow if desired. Make each leaf different to add interest.

Flowers - Basecoat Moon Yellow, add touches of Beautiful Burgundy, Golden Halo or mixtures of Beautiful Burgundy and Country Blue. Spatter with Beautiful Burgundy and Hunter Green.

Box - Sponge the wide band with Patina Green, let dry. Spray with sealer. Brush on a coat of Heavenly Grey, wipe off immediately. Let dry 1 hour. Spray with 2 or 3 coats of sealer.

Lettering - Make lettering with Green marker.

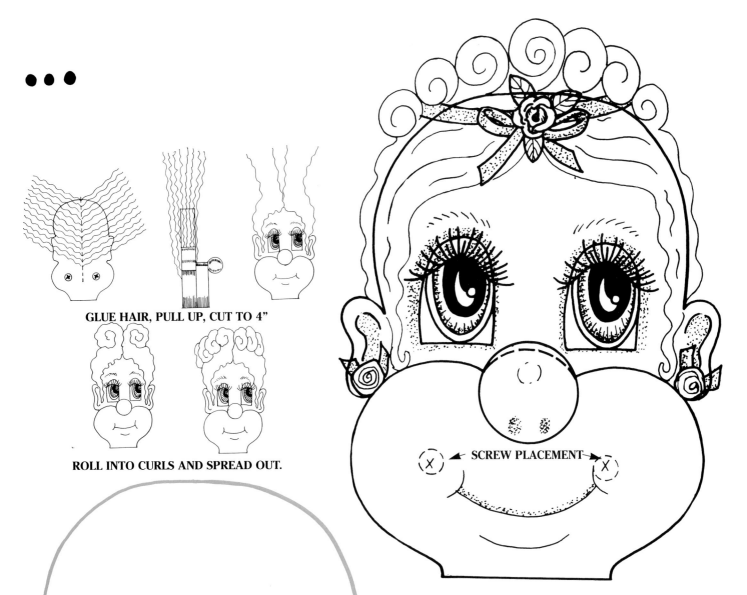

GLUE HAIR, PULL UP, CUT TO 4"

ROLL INTO CURLS AND SPREAD OUT.

← **SCREW PLACEMENT** →

'Mom' Glasses Holder

PHOTO ON PAGE 128
by Jean Gaston

MATERIALS:

5" x 9" piece of ¾" White pine
2⅝" x 4" wood oval
1" wood ball, 1" of ⅛" dowel
12" of ½" Burgundy picot satin ribbon
Small silk rosebud with leaves
2 Pink ¼" ribbon roses
White curly doll hair
Acrylic paint - Rose, Ivory, Black,
  White, Brown, Red, Blue
Paintbrushes - ¾" flat, ½" flat,
  #0 fine liner, #6 blender
Two 1" drywall screws, Sandpaper
Water base varnish
Brown paper bag
Drill and 2 bits (⅛" and size of screws)
Scroll saw
Sponge, White glue

INSTRUCTIONS:

Trace and transfer patterns to wood,
cut out. Sand all wood pieces smooth.
Drill ¼" deep holes for screws in back
of head. Drill ⅛" holes ½" deep in nose
and cheek piece.

PAINT:

Head, cheeks, nose - mix ½ Rose and ½
Ivory, let dry.
Oval - Black.
  Rub pieces with a crumpled Brown
  paper bag.
  Repeat painting and rubbing.
  Transfer painting pattern.
Edges, under eyes, ears - shade by dip-
ping brush in water, blotting and dip-
ping in Rose and blending through
brush on paper.
Eyes - White.
  Iris, ring - Blue.
  Pupil - Black, highlight with White
    comma and dot.

Details - Black with fine liner.
Outside edge of iris - shade with
    thinned Black.
Details - outline with Black.
Eyelashes, eyebrows - Black.
Cheeks - shade Brown.
Upper lip - shade Red.
Blush - mix thinned Red with Rose,
    dampen sponge, squeeze excess and
    dip in paint. Blot sponge on paper
    until almost dry, lightly press on
    cheeks.
Nostrils - shade Red.

ASSEMBLE: Glue dowel in nose and
cheek hole. Screw head to cheeks. Glue
base on bottom. Seal with varnish.
Spread and glue hair across back of
head, pull up and trim to 4". Tie 10" of
ribbon around curls and in a bow. Glue
silk rose on bow. Cut remaining ribbon
in half, glue ribbon pieces and ribbon
roses on ears.

Collin's Guardian Angel

Renuzit Guardian Angel

PHOTO ON PAGE 128
by Judy Lindquist

MATERIALS:

Renuzit bottle air freshener
Warm & Natural cotton batting
6" heart and 1" round White crocheted doilies
Mini curl doll hair
Gold wire to tie bow for wings
18" of ⅜" and 1¾ yards of ⅟₁₆" White satin ribbon
1 yard of #40 Sheer Gold wired ribbon
3" grapevine wreath
1¾" wood ball knob
#2 Black Pigma pen, Pinking shears
Brown craft paper, White graphite paper
Magic Melt Princess Low Temp Glue and oval glue sticks
DecoArt Paints (Titanium White, Country Red, Flesh Tone, Wedgewood Blue, Lamp Black)
Loew-Cornell brushes (#1 liner #7350 series, #4 Fabric Dye series FAB)
White So Soft Dimensional Fabric Writer
Krylon Matte Sealer #1311

INSTRUCTIONS

Paint - Paint ball knob Flesh, let dry. Transfer face pattern using graphite paper. Paint eyes White and pupils Blue. Outline eyes with Black. Dot a White highlight in top right of each eye. Paint mouth Red. Drybrush cheeks Red. Seal with Krylon.

Dress - Using pinking shears, cut 12" and 8" circles from Brown paper. Cut two circles of batting ¼" larger than the paper circles. With Black marker, draw stitching lines around circles ¼" from edges. Place the paper circles on top of the batting circles and glue together making sure ¼" of batting shows all the way around. Cut each circle in half. Roll the small half circles into cones for arms, glue seam. For the skirt, roll one large half circle into a cone to fit to top of Renuzit bottle. Glue skirt seam, glue skirt to top of bottle. Trim top of cone flat with top of bottle, glue on head. Glue arms to sides of angel making sure all seams are in the back.

Hair - Cut a slit from the outside edge to center of doily and position over shoulders. Glue at neck. Tie ⅜" ribbon bow and glue on neck. Glue hair on head. Use a lot of hair on the top and

pull it up in a big bob, tie with ⅟₁₆" ribbon to hold in place. Fit the wreath over the bob and glue to hair. Glue 1" doily to the left.

Finish - Tie a bow with Gold ribbon leaving 4" tails. Glue to back of head. Shape ribbon into full wings. Spray entire angel with Krylon, spraying hair more heavily. To personalize your angel, cut banner from Brown paper with pinking shears. Draw stitching lines around edge with Black marker. Write name with White fabric writer.

Red Plaid Sachet

PHOTO ON PAGE 129
by Laura & Melissa Rafson

FINISHED SIZE: 4¾" square

MATERIALS:

Two 4¾" squares of Red/White plaid fabric
Two 4¾" squares of White tulle
3¼" White Battenburg lace doily
25" of ⅟₁₆" White satin ribbon
Four ⅜" Red ribbon roses with Green leaves
White and Red thread
Potpourri
Tacky glue
Fray check

INSTRUCTIONS:

Iron fabric squares. Center and pin doily on front of one square. Zigzag stitch around edges. Very carefully cut away fabric behind doily. Stack and pin 2 pieces of tulle to wrong side of front square.

With right sides of squares together, sew a ¼" seam around edges leaving a small opening on one side. Turn right side out.

Cut ribbon into four 6¼" pieces. Make 4 bows and fray check the ends. Stitch bows on corners referring to photo. Glue a ribbon rose in center of each bow. Stuff with potpourri. Stitch opening shut.

On backside, cut away fabric inside stitching

Denim & Lace Sachet
PHOTO ON PAGE 129
by Laura & Melissa Rafson
FINISHED SIZE: 4¾" square
MATERIALS:

Two 4¾" squares of denim
3¼" White Battenburg lace doily
12" of White ¾" crocheted lace
Eight 5mm pearls
⅝" White ribbon rose
White and Blue thread
Potpourri

INSTRUCTIONS:

Iron fabric squares. Center and pin doily on front of one square. Zigzag stitch around edges.

Cut crocheted lace into four 3" pieces. Referring to photo, pin and sew lace across corners of fabric. Sew pearls around doily and ribbon rose in center.

With right sides of squares together, sew a ¼" seam around edges leaving a small opening on one side. Turn right side out and stuff with potpourri. Stitch opening shut.

Frame with Blue Fabric Mat
PHOTO ON PAGE 129
by Helen Rafson

MATERIALS:

5" x 7" wood frame
3½" x 5" photo
5 colors of Blue denim and/or chambray fabric
12" x 12" of muslin
Two 5" x 7" pieces of cardboard
Batting
Masking tape
White glue

INSTRUCTIONS:

Cut two 1½" x 12" strips of each Blue fabric. Place first strip right side up on muslin. With right sides facing, place second strip on top of first strip. Sew a ¼" seam on one side. Iron seam to one side then fold down strip. Repeat with remaining strips.

Trace pattern on one piece of cardboard and cut out oval. Cut 5" x 7" of batting, glue on cardboard and cut out oval. Place batting side on back of pieced fabric slanting seams in the direction of the lines. Center cardboard on pieced fabric

and cut out a fabric rectangle 1" wider on each side than the cardboard. Fold excess fabric to back of cardboard, trim off corners and glue in place.

On back mark a ⅜" seam inside oval and cut out. Slash seam, iron to back and glue down. Let dry. Position photo behind oval opening and tape down. Insert mat into frame and back with second piece of cardboard.

Bunny Angel
PHOTO ON PAGE 130
by Kathy Krystosik

MATERIALS:

Two 3" x 1¼" wood hearts (wings)
1¾" wood ball knob (head)
Two ¾" wood ball knobs (hands)
2" of ³⁄₁₆" dowel
6" of ¼" White Picot satin ribbon
24" of ⅛" White satin ribbon
12" of ¹⁄₁₆" Blue satin ribbon
3" x 5" of paper canvas
10" of 19 gauge wire
Raffia
Small flat basket with handle

BUNNY ANGEL PATTERN

Dried flowers and Spanish moss
Mauve and Blue wide paper twist
Cosmetic blush
Clear satin spray finish
DECOART PAINTS:

Buttermilk, Mink Tan, Mauve, Ebony Black, Snow White, Navy Blue, Williamsburg Blue
INSTRUCTIONS:

Ears - Trace ear pattern and transfer to paper canvas twice, cut out. Gather bottom of each ear, glue to head.
Paint:
Head, hands, wings - Buttermilk.
Transfer face pattern.
Eyes - Snow White.
Irises - Williamsburg Blue, outline Navy Blue.
Highlights - dot Snow White.
Pupils - Ebony Black.
Lashes - Mink Tan.
Nose, mouth - Mauve.
Cheeks - brush with blush.

Assemble - Glue hearts together to form wings. Spray head, hands and wings with satin finish. Glue dowel into hole at bottom of head. Glue ¾" ball knobs on ends of wire to form arms and hands.

Dress - From Blue paper twist cut 11" x 24" for skirt and 10" x 5" for sleeves, from Mauve paper twist cut 9" x 24" for overskirt. Fold overskirt in half 4 times, cut scallops along one long edge. Overlap short ends of skirt, overskirt and sleeves and glue seams. Gather and glue skirt around dowel ¼" below head. Gather and glue Mauve overskirt on top of Blue skirt.

Arms - Slip wire and hands through sleeves. Gather ½" from each ends of sleeves and glue against hands. Glue ⅛" White ribbon over gathers. Glue center of arms to back of angel.

Finish - Cut a slit from outer edge to center of doily, place around neck and glue edges together at back. Tie remaining ⅛" White ribbon into a bow with long streamers and glue to neck. Glue Blue ribbon around head for headband. Tie a tiny Blue bow, glue to band. Loop ¼" White ribbon, glue to wings for hanger. Glue wings to back of angel.

Flower Basket - Arrange flowers and moss in basket. Tie a raffia bow, glue to front of basket. Glue hands together with arms holding basket.

SERVING TRAY PATTERN

Serving Tray

PHOTO ON PAGE 130
by Margaret Hanson

MATERIALS:
9⅞" x 15⅞" wood serving tray
Almond acrylic spray paint
Scraps of assorted fabrics
   (refer to photo for colors)
¼ yard of HeatnBond® fusible webbing
Assorted buttons
Scraps of lace and ribbon
52" of ¼" Green ribbon

Embroidery floss, Darning needle
Mini-satin roses
Small beads
Charms
Plexiglass cut to fit bottom of tray
Black fine-tip Pigma Pen®
Tacky Glue

INSTRUCTIONS:

Spray tray and let dry completely. Using a blow dryer will speed up drying time. Tray must be completely dry to fuse fabric to it. Trace pattern pieces and transfer to paper side of HeatnBond.

Apply HeatnBond to fabrics and cut out pattern pieces. Place pieces on tray. Fuse pieces in place following manufacturers instructions.

Thread needle with 10" of floss and glue needle onto hand of lady on left. Cut a 3" square from fabric. Crumple square and glue between ladies' hands. Glue lace, ribbon, buttons, beads, charms and floss pieces referring to photo. Glue ¼" ribbon around outside of tray.

Place plexiglass in bottom of tray.

Tiny Angel Pin

PHOTO ON PAGE 131
by Kimberly Thomas

WINGS

MATERIALS:

6" of Ecru gathered lace
6" of 1/16" Blue satin ribbon
2" of Gold stardust garland
Tacky glue, GOOP glue
9/16" wood bead (head)
Two 1/4" wood beads (arms)
5/8" x 5/8" wood mini bean pot cup (body)
1" of Light Brown curly chenille hair
Blank card, Toothpick, Small sharp scissors
2 Gold butterfly conchos, 1 Gold pin back
Pink cosmetic blush, Black acrylic paint
Heavy-duty nylon thread, Needle

INSTRUCTIONS:

Face - Glue head to bottom of bean pot. Rub blush on cheeks with fingertip. Dip toothpick in fresh pool of Black paint and dot eyes.

Wings - Referring to diagram, overlap conchos and glue with GOOP, let dry.

Dress - Run a gathering stitch along gathered edge of lace. Pull tightly around doll's neck, tie off. Even gathers and glue at back. Referring to photo, glue dress to body where arms will be placed. Glue arms to doll. Tie a ribbon bow and glue to angel's neck.

Hair - Cut chenille hair into 1/16" pieces and glue to head with tacky glue. Make a 1/2" circle with garland and glue on hair.

Assemble - Glue angel to center of conchos. Glue pin on back near top of wings.

Card - Trace angel saying provided, flip tracing over and rub back of letters with a pencil. Place saying in lower portion of card. Trace saying using a ballpoint pen and pressing firmly. Remove tracing and go over letters with Black marker. To attach pin to the card cut small circles and the line between them 1 5/8" from the top edge. Pin angel to card.

Autumn Clothespin Angel

PHOTO ON PAGE 131
by Nancy Bell Anderson

MATERIALS:

Round clothespin
2 craft picks
Small round Woodsie
Red, Blue, White, and Brown
    permanent markers
Pink acrylic paint
Paintbrush
Small piece of mohair doll hair
3 1/4" x 7" piece of Red calico fabric
Sewing needle and thread
Tacky glue
Acorn cap
4 maple seeds
Dried flowers

INSTRUCTIONS:

Draw face on clothespin. Cut craft picks 1" from round ends for arms. Sew running stitches on one 7" edge of fabric, place around clothespin, pull stitches tight and tie off. Glue arms in folds of dress at shoulders. Glue hair on head and acorn cap on hair. Glue maple seeds for wings and flowers in hand. Glue clothespin angel on Woodsie.

Cut small circles and the line between them 1 5/8" from the edge of card.

1 5/8" from the edge

Just like Angels from heaven above, This little Angel was made with love. Where ever you go, and what ever you do Wear this little Angel to watch over you.

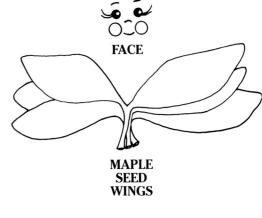

FACE

MAPLE
SEED
WINGS

Friendship Bags

Often a meaningful little book, a collection of poems or a thoughtful memento can be awarded special value by presenting it in a wrapper embellished by hand. Simply use an inexpensive bag then decorate it with colorful felt, fabric, buttons, stickers, gift cards, ribbons or raffia. The result...instant personalization.

Lani, Kristy & Suzanne

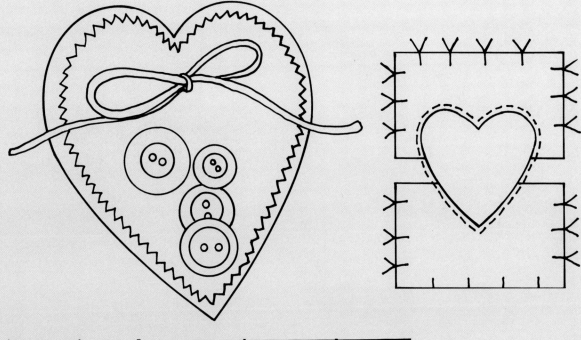

Hands to work,
Hearts to God.

Gift Tags

Photocopy the tags on these pages for your personal use. They make wonderful additions to special handmade 'Friendship Gifts'.

Circle of Friendship

    The words 'gift' and 'handmade' are connected by love. The thought that goes into a handmade gift adds true value. A store-bought present is something anyone can give at the last minute; a personalized gift requires prior thought, careful planning, and valuable time.

    As a child, I eagerly looked forward to unique handmade gifts that appeared on birthdays, Christmas and special days. Mother encouraged everyone to give items that could be hand embellished or personalized. Even when handmade didn't turn out perfect Mother simply assured us, "Perfect things look like they are made by machines, small imperfections let everyone know that this valuable piece is crafted by hand."

    Friendship gifts celebrate heartfelt thoughts. I hope you will feel the sincerity and love that went into each special item.

"I can't remember a time when I wasn't making something special for somebody" ...Julie McGuffee

"When I make a gift by hand it is given from my heart and created with my talent and my time"...Barbara Burnett

"Being able to make valued gifts inexpensively has always been important to me"...Virginia Tucker

Friend to Friend

When this you see, remember me.

"Making presents by hand allows me to personalize gifts for my friends"...Linda Rocamontes

"For me, love is and always will be giving or receiving a thoughtful handmade gift"...Jean Kievlan

"I have always felt that when I give a handmade gift it is an expression of love straight from my heart"...Delores Frantz

"Crafting has always been part of my life. Giving or receiving handmade gifts is a special treat"...Kim Ballor

"I enjoy giving a very special part of myself to the friends I cherish when I make gifts for them"...Donna Thomason

Index of Friendship Projects and Designers

Note: Instructions for friendship gift projects follow each chapter.

I want to extend a special Thank You to the talented crafters who contributed their love and creativity to **Friendship Gifts**.

Every time I opened a package to reveal the special heartfelt gift project inside, I felt the warm glow of love and caring that went into the thought and creation behind it. Each day when I read the special meaning behind the gift, I felt the special relationship that inspired that gift.

As each year goes by, I learn to appreciate friends more and value their caring hearts.

Suzanne